European Parliament Elections after Eastern Enlargement

This book reflects on the questions raised by the European Election Study 2004 whose analytical focus was on the legitimacy of EU politics after Eastern enlargement. It also assesses the dynamics and the contents of the campaign, on the determinants of the extremely low turnout in the new countries, and on the reasons of voter choice in West and East.

The book also examines the first European Parliament election after the post-communist countries of Eastern Europe joined the European Union. The central question is: what has changed? Are the voters in the new member countries different and if so, why? Did the Union suffer from a loss of democratic legitimacy after Eastern enlargement?

Each chapter is empirical-analytical; most are based on the post-election surveys of the group that were conducted in all but one of the 25 member countries, others focus on the results of content analyses of news media and party manifestos.

This book was published as a special issue of the *Journal of European Integration*.

Hermann Schmitt is a research fellow of the MZES and a Privatdozent for Political Science at the University of Mannheim. He was a visiting professor at the University of Michigan (1996-7), Science Po Paris (2001-2), the Australian National University (2003), the IAS in Vienna (2005), and the UAM in Madrid (2008). He received his doctorate from the University of Duisburg, and his first habilitation from the Free University of Berlin. He has been participating in a number of comparative projects; perhaps most important is his involvement, from 1979 onwards, in the series of European Election Studies. He is the author and editor of numerous books and articles on electoral behaviour in multilevel-systems and on political parties and political representation in the EU.

T0316054

European Parliament Elections after Eastern Enlargement

Edited by Hermann Schmitt

Routledge
Taylor & Francis Group

LONDON AND NEW YORK

First published 2010 by Routledge
2 Park Square, Milton Park, Abingdon, Oxon, OX14 4RN

Simultaneously published in the USA and Canada
by Routledge
711 Third Avenue, New York, NY 10017

Routledge is an imprint of the Taylor & Francis Group, an informa business

First issued in paperback 2012

© 2010 Taylor & Francis

Typeset in Sabon by Value Chain, India

British Library Cataloguing in Publication Data
A catalogue record for this book is available from the British Library

ISBN 13: 978-0-415-55675-0 (hbk)

ISBN 13: 978-0-415-50948-0 (pbk)

CONTENTS

Introduction

HERMANN SCHMITT

MZES, University of Mannheim, Mannheim, Germany

ABSTRACT   The present contribution to the scholarly knowledge about European Parliament (EP) elections essentially assembles analyses of the data of the *2004 European Election Study*. Due to the very nature of large-scale cross-national comparative survey research, it will only be published shortly after the 2009 European Parliament election. As it would certainly be inadequate to ignore the fact that another European election took place just before publication, this introduction to the analyses that follow will start out with a first inspection of the results of this most recent European election — the election of the members of the European Parliament in June 2009. The main question we will be asking is about the persistence of the 'second-order' character of these elections: are the 2009 European Parliament election results in line with our expectations about European Parliament elections as second-order national elections as laid out originally by Reif and Schmitt (1980) and restated and refined in a large number of subsequent publications? The second part of this introduction will then go on and do what every introduction does: briefly present the contributions that follow.

The 2009 Election to the European Parliament: Still Second-Order?

European Parliament elections have been described as second-order national elections (SOEs). This judgement was inspired by the fact that the national political arena has been so much more important than that of the European Union — at least in the early years of direct elections to the European Parliament. Under these circumstances, turnout was expected to be lower in SOEs; government parties were expected to lose votes in SOEs, and those losses were predicted to follow the national electoral cycle; small parties were expected to win and ideologically extreme or polar parties were also expected to win relative to their previous first-order election (FOE) result (Reif and Schmitt 1980). A re-examination of these aggregate predictions at the occasion of the 2004 EP election broadly confirmed them. The one major qualification to this conclusion was that things at the time worked out differently in the new Eastern member countries (Schmitt

Correspondence Address: Hermann Schmitt, MZES, University of Mannheim, D-68131 Mannheim, Germany. E-mail: Hermann.Schmitt@mzes.uni-mannheim.de

2005). A tentative explanation of these deviant findings referred to the relative fluidity of the party and electoral systems in the post-communist democracies of Eastern Europe.

We are interested here in the second-order character of European Parliament elections five years later. Was turnout in the 2009 European Parliament elections again lower if compared to the previous national FOE in the respective country? Did government parties lose and was the magnitude of those possible losses governed by the relative position of an EP election in the national electoral cycle? And last but not least, did small parties — and ideologically more extreme parties — two qualities which go together quite regularly — do systematically better in European Parliament elections?

Turnout was Lower

Turnout is expected to be lower in second-order elections generally, and in European Parliament elections in particular. One line of reasoning refers to the comparatively lower level of political mobilisation and stimulation (e.g. Campbell 1960). Specifically for EP elections, an alternative hypothesis has been proposed which stipulates that low turnout is a function of a lack of support for and legitimacy of the EU level of government (e.g. Blondel et al. 1998). While this second reasoning has found little empirical support so far (e.g. Van der Eijk and Schmitt 2009), it can not be ruled out as a matter of principle. A third plausible motivation for low turnout in SOE is dissatisfaction with one's last FOE vote choice (Schmitt et al. 2009). But we are not looking at the motivations of individual turnout decisions here — this has to wait for future analyses due to the non-availability of survey data at the time of writing. What we can do instead is to compare aggregate turnout levels for national first-order elections with those for the EP election of 2009.

Figure 1 shows that turnout was again lower in the European Parliament election of June 2009 compared to the preceding national first-order election. Belgium and Luxembourg are the only two exceptions among the 27 member countries. There turnout is about at the same level as in national first-order elections. This is due to the Belgian system of compulsory voting and the fact that, in Luxembourg, European Parliament elections are held concurrently with national parliament elections.

In all other 25 EU member-countries, turnout was lower than it was in the previous FOE. How much lower it was depends to a considerable degree on the turnout level that tends to be achieved in a FOE (as indicated by an R square of 0.68). This is to say that low FOE turnout rates (as found in Lithuania, Poland, Romania and Slovakia) produce record-low EP participation rates, while high FOE turnout rates (as in Cyprus, Denmark, Italy and Malta) go hand in hand with relatively high EP turnout levels. Note however the asymmetric positioning of the regression slope relative to the (dotted) diagonal of the graph: this indicates that low turnout countries suffer somewhat more from the SOE turnout loss than high turnout countries do.

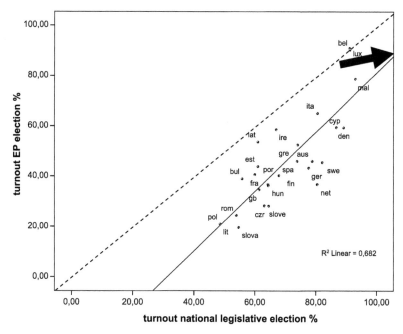

Figure 1. Turnout is Lower in the 2009 European Parliament Elections.
Note: Displayed are percentages of the electorate turnout.

Government Parties Lost — Most of Them at Least

Logically, there are two and only two reasons why government parties can be expected to lose in SOE — one strategic, the other sincere. The strategic motivation for abandoning one's FOE choice of a government party has to do with its performance since the FOE: voters might be dissatisfied with it and either abstain (the softer signal) or switch to another party (the harder signal) as a result of it. The sincere motivation of switching to other than the government party that a voter had chosen at the previous FOE would again be arena-specific: a dissatisfaction with the arena-specific — i.e. EU — policies of the previous vote choice at the time of the SOE (Schmitt et al. 2009).

Again, because of the lack of suitable survey data at the time of writing, we cannot dig into the motivations of individual vote choices. However, we can and will inspect the distributions of 27 member countries' aggregate results. Figure 2 shows how national government parties did in the European Parliament election of June 2009. Relative to their last FOE, national governments lost. There are only two clear exceptions to this rule: the governments of Poland and Finland did better in the EP election than they did in the previous FOE.

At the time of the 2009 EP election, the semi-presidential system of Poland was stuck in a situation of divided government in which an outright EU-sceptical president Lech Kaczynski (Law and Justice, PiS) was confronting a somehow more EU-phoric prime minister Donald Tusk

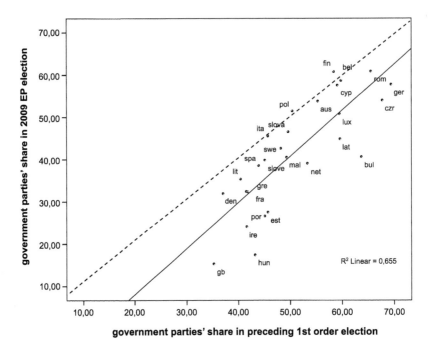

Figure 2. Government Parties Lose the 2009 European Parliament Elections.
Note: Displayed are proportions of government parties in the valid vote.

(Civic Platform, PO). This battle was on since Tusk won the last national legislative election, and the slight increase (in the proportion of valid votes) of Tusk in the EP election can perhaps be understood as a sincere expression of preference among the electorate for co-operation rather than confrontation with the European Union.

The situation in Finland was similar in a way. Here as well, the strongly Euro-positive National Coalition Party won while the senior government partner — the Centre Party — lost votes. This could be understood again as a sincere expression of support for a more Euro-positive policy of Finland.

Examples of sizable defeats of national government parties are more numerous. We will pick just three of them, all concerning a socialist- or labour-led government. The British Labour party, the Hungarian Socialist Party (MSZP), and the Bulgarian Socialist Party (BSP) all suffered a disastrous defeat which, in the case of Bulgaria, has already led to a change of the leading national government party. The political reasons for such near-collapses are likely to be domestic rather than European. But again, micro-level survey evidence will be needed to arrive at a firmer conclusion here.

Did Government Losses Follow the National Electoral Cycle?

National electoral cycles are referring to a particular pattern of government popularity. Shortly after a FOE, government popularity is expected to increase even beyond the level of support received in the election ('honeymoon' or post-electoral euphoria), in order to more or less continuously decrease until sometime after midterm, and to rise again to a new level of support at the next FOE. This characteristic pattern of government popularity has been successful in predicting the level of support national governments manage to receive in European Parliament elections that all take place, in the various member countries, at a different point in time of the national electoral cycle (e.g. Reif 1984; Marsh 1998; Schmitt 2005).

Did government losses in the 2009 European Parliament elections again follow the national electoral cycle? The short answer is no. As Figure 3 demonstrates, this time we do not find a trace of a cyclical pattern in government losses, even if we control for possible distorting effects in the political makeup of the political systems of the new Eastern member countries of the European Union. All we can say on the basis of this joint distribution is that government losses tend to be graver the later an EP election is held in a national legislative period. Based on an R square of 0.313, however, even this generalisation is far from deterministic.

What does it mean, then, that there is no cyclical element left in the evolution of support for government parties in European Parliament elections? It may mean two different things. First, government support in the EU member countries might not follow a cyclical pattern anymore. The evolution of government popularity as identified in some sort of monthly barometer

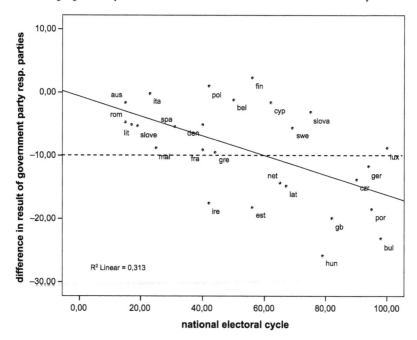

Figure 3. National Government Losses as a Function of the Timing of EP Elections in the National Electoral Cycle.

Note: Displayed are differences in the proportions of government parties in the valid vote according to the position of the EP election in the national electoral cycle.

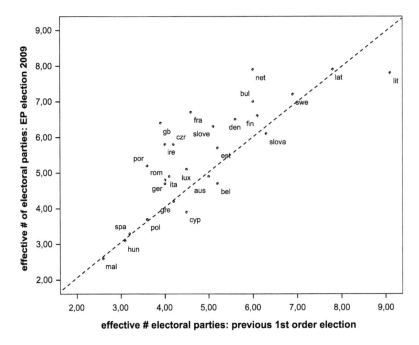

Figure 4. Small Parties did Better in the 2009 European Parliament Elections.

surveys would be useful to test this proposition. There is a second possible explanation which — should it be confirmed — would be very consequential for our understanding of the nature of European Parliament elections. It goes like this: the absence of cyclical elements in national government losses may also mean that EP electoral behaviour is less determined by national politics, and that these European elections are therefore gradually losing their second-order character. Again, we need micro-level survey evidence to investigate this second possible explanation.

Did Small Parties Gain Relative to their Previous FOE Result?

Because there is less at stake in European Parliament elections, there is also less of an incentive to vote strategically — i.e. to choose another than the most preferred party. Strategic voting favours larger parties over smaller ones because they can more effectively contribute to government formation. However, government formation — in the conventional sense at least –is not an issue in European Parliament elections. This is why small parties are expected to win in European Parliament elections relative to their last FOE result (Schmitt et al. 2009). We compare the effective number of electoral parties (according to Laakso and Taagepera 1979) for the EP election result and the preceding FOE result, and expect that the index is systematically higher for the EP election.

This expectation is barely confirmed by the results of the 2009 European Parliament elections. In a few countries — Belgium, Lithuania and Malta —

we find hints in the opposite direction, that is: that big parties were doing better. Moreover, in 11 other countries a party's electoral fortunes in EP elections are hardly affected by their size, and the effective number of electoral parties does not differ much between EP elections and the preceding FOE. This leaves us with 13 countries in which small parties did substantially better in EP elections, just below the simple majority of EU member countries. This is again an indication that the second order election model of European Parliament elections is somehow put into question by these 2009 election results — some of its theoretical underpinnings at least, if not the whole model.

The 2004 Study

The 2009 European Election Study[1] is currently being conducted, and full results will be available by the end of the year. The analyses that follow are therefore all based, in total or in part, on the findings of the 2004 European Election Study. European Election Studies have been conducted from the very first direct election of the members of the European Parliament in 1979 onwards (with the one exception of 1984). All of them were 'more' than election studies in the narrow sense, that is: more than just a series of surveys among eligible voters. Some of these studies have also included one or more party elite surveys, be it among constituency candidates, members of the European Parliament (MEPs), or members of national parliaments (MNPs); other studies have shared a particular focus on the campaign, either through participant observation or quantitative analyses of media content; last but not least, the election manifestos of political parties have been collected and content-analysed, for all election years. The 2004 study specifically included a campaign study, a manifesto analysis, and a series of post-election surveys in 24 of the then 25 member-countries of the European Union.

The latter data collection exercise, the post-election survey, was truly extraordinary on several accounts. To start with, our efforts to acquire central funding for this most expensive part of any election study failed. A research proposal was submitted to the European Commission under the 6th Framework Programme which, unfortunately, did not find the congenial reviewers that it undoubtedly would have deserved. In early 2004 we decided to try and conduct a 'de-central' post-election survey in as many member-countries of the European Union as possible — de-central in the sense that local study directors in each of the member-countries would be in charge of fund raising, questionnaire translation, data collection and deposition, and reporting. Following the theoretical guidance of the unfortunate research proposal, a common questionnaire was drafted by the co-ordination of the study at the *Mannheimer Zentrum für Europäische Sozialforschung* (MZES), and discussed and revised by a meeting of all local study directors convened at the MZES in Mannheim.

In early 2004, we would have considered it a big success if we were able to cover half of the member countries of the Union this way. It turned out that we were able to cover all of them — with the one exception of Malta were we could not identify somebody interested in this co-operation. These local teams,[2] numbering 24 in total, contributed in the shared understanding that if they were able to deliver their part, they would receive all other national studies in return plus, after a while, an integrated data-file and codebook[3] as an indispensable facilitator of comparative analyses.

In addition to these surveys, the 2004 study contributed to and benefited from the research programme of CONNEX, a Network of Excellence for Research into multi-level EU governance funded under the 6th Framework Programme of the European Commission. CONNEX facilitated data integration by paying a modest stipend to Mathew Loveless while he finished his dissertation and worked on the study at the MZES in Mannheim from mid 2004 to mid 2005. CONNEX was also extremely helpful in funding several of our authors' meetings, not least the one in which most of the contributions that are now assembled here were presented as first drafts of their papers.[4]

The Analyses

The objective of this study is to assess the effect of Eastern enlargement on various aspects of the input legitimacy of European Union politics. The contributions that are assembled here can be grouped in three sections: a first one dealing with East–West differences in citizens' attitudes towards European integration and towards one another; a second with the EU party system and the election campaign after Eastern enlargement; and a third with electoral participation and vote choices in the 2004 election to the European Parliament. This last section is by far the largest of the three.

The section on *European attitudes* presents two analyses. Garry and Tilley deal with the question of whether EU support in the East is based on different sources than in the West. In particular, two hypotheses are derived and tested. One of them states that the economy is more important for Eastern EU support, while the other states that democracy is more important. Garry and Tilley's analysis corroborates the first of these expectations while it refutes the second.

Scheuer and Schmitt ask whether the citizens of the enlarged European Union share a common political identity. EU enlargement is here not restricted to its latest round but conceived as a continuous process. The results of this analysis suggest that (a) yes, there is a sense of community among the citizens of the EU and (b) the farther away one gets from the core of the Union in both geographical and temporal terms, the weaker this sense of community becomes.

The section on the *European party system* again presents two analyses. Schmitt and Thomassen deal with the EU party system before and after enlargement. They investigate whether and how the process of Eastern enlargement has altered the EU party system. Comparing party placements on the two main dimensions of political contestation in the EU — the left–right dimension and the integration–independence dimension — it finds that Eastern enlargement did surprisingly little to the format of the EU party system and the stature of its political groups, both regarding their distinctiveness and their cohesion.

Van der Brug and Fennema in their contribution analyse whether support for radical right parties (both in the West and the East of the European Union) is caused by different factors than support for 'other' parties. Based on EES 2004 data, their main finding is that smallest-distance voting according to the left–right logic is somewhat less important for supporting these parties as compared to others. As neither democracy nor EU nor government dissatisfaction plays an important role in explaining radical support for right parties, they also reject the protest-vote hypothesis as a potential explanation of radical right party support.

The section on *electoral participation and party choice* presents the bulk of the contributions, five altogether. Franklin and Wessels examine the factors that cause low turnout in European Parliament elections. They propose that low turnout is a function of three deficits: a deficit of political community, a deficit of institutional effectiveness and a deficit of mobilisation. Together with the well known context characteristics of compulsory voting and the national electoral cycle, these three individual-level predictors are found to explain turnout levels quite well. The main conclusion here is that post-communist and Western EU citizens are following the same cues in much the same way.

Marsh, in his contribution, investigates the reasons for vote switching in the 2004 election to the European Parliament relative to the previous national election. He reviews and tests three major theories of vote switching in less important elections, and finds support for most of the predictions in most of them. What remains on the agenda, according to him, is the question of intra-coalition switching, and the role that partisanship plays in all of this.

Clark and Rohrschneider analyse the same question with a focus on second-order election models. They propose two oppositite hypotheses: a transfer hypothesis (voters transfer national political concerns to EP voting decisions) and a 1st-order hypothesis (voters evaluate the EU on its own performance terms). Support for both models is found. In the narrow election context, the transfer hypothesis receives considerable support. In a broader perspective, however, voters clearly separate the two levels and evaluate each on its own terms.

Freire, Costa Lobo and Magalhaes in their contribution, finally demonstrate that survey data collected on the occasion of European Parliament elections are relevant for the study of electoral behaviour more generally. They examine whether the ideological location of citizens — in terms of left–right self-placement — has a different impact on the vote in different types of democratic regime by controlling for three other factors hypothesized to make a difference: the permissiveness of the electoral system; the clarity of policy alternatives provided by the party system; and the particular type of party alignments. Their major finding is that the impact of left–right self-placements is a stronger predictor of the vote the more polarized a party system is.

All in all, this collection of scholarly work that grew out of the 2004 European Election Study delineates the limited but visible impact that

Eastern enlargement of the European Union had on aspects of the input legitimacy of EU politics. In terms of EU attitudes and support, the economy seems to play a different role in the East than in the West; in addition, it has been shown that mutual trust and a sense of community take time to develop and grow — a fact which will be leaving the 'New East' of the European Union behind for some time to come. The EU party system and EP election campaigns seem hardly altered by Eastern enlargement, and determinants of electoral participation and party choice are much the same here and there. It is just that the context factors that stimulate or facilitate the one or the other differ more or less systematically between Western Europe and the post-communist East.

Notes

1. The 2009 EES (European Election Study) is funded under the 7th Framework Programme of the European Commission as a Design Infrastructure, and coordinated by the Robert Schuman Centre of the European University Institute in Florence.
2. The national study directors were: Günther Ogris (Austria), Marc Swyngedouw and Lieven de Winter (Belgium), James Tilley (Britain) and John Garry (Northern Ireland), Bambos Papageorgiou (Cyprus), Lukas Linek (Czech Republic), Jorgen Goul Andersen (Denmark), Alan Sikk and Vello Pettai (Estonia), Mikko Maatila and Tapio Raunio (Finland), Pascal Perrineau and Bruno Cautres (France), Hermann Schmitt and Andreas Wüst (Germany), Ilias Nikolakopoulos and Eftichia Teperoglou (Greece), Gabor Toka (Hungary), Michael Marsh (Ireland), Renato Mannheimer and Roberto Biorcio (Italy), Ilze Koroleva (Latvia), Algis Krupavicius (Lithuania), Patrick Dumont (Luxembourg), Cees van der Eijk (The Netherlands), Radoslaw Markowski (Poland), Pedro Magalhaes (Portugal), Olga Gyarfasova (Slovakia), Niko Tos (Slovenia), Juan Diez Nicolas (Spain), and Sören Holmberg (Sweden). For more information on the specifics of the 2004 surveys, see http://www.europeanelectionstudies.net.
3. In the spring of 2009, a second edition of this integrated data-file and codebook was published which corrects a few inconsistencies present in the first edition and adds a number of constructed variables that might be useful in further analyses (Schmitt, Loveless et al. 2009 with an analysis of interview mode effects contributed by Till Weber. The data-file and codebook is available from the EES homepage at http://www.europeanelectionstudies.net.
4. This meeting took place in late spring of 2006 at the Institute for Social Research of the University of Lisbon, Portugal. It was organised by Marina Costa Lobo which is most gratefully acknowledged.

References

Blondel, J., R. Sinnott, and P. Svensson. 1998. *People and Parliament in the European Union.* Oxford: Clarendon Press.

Campbell, A. 1960. Surge and decline. A study of electoral change. *Public Opinion Quarterly* 24, no. 3: 397–418.

Laakso, M., and R. Taagepera. 1979. Effective number of parties: A measure with application to West Europe. *Comparative Political Studies* 12, no. 1: 3–27.

Marsh, M. 1998. Testing the second-order election model after four European Parliament elections. *British Journal for Political Science* 28, no. 4: 591–607.

Reif, K. 1984. National electoral cycles and European elections. *Electoral Studies* 3, no. 3: 244–55.

Reif, K., and H. Schmitt. 1980. Nine second order national elections: A conceptual framework for the analysis of European election results. *European Journal of Political Research* 8, no. 1: 3–44.

Schmitt, H. 2005. The European Parliament election of June 2004: Still second order? *West European Politics* 28, no. 3: 650–79.

Schmitt, H., M. Loveless, D. Braun, and S. Adam, eds. 2009. *European Election Study 2004: Design, data description, and documentation.* 2nd ed. Mannheim: MZES, University of Mannheim.

Schmitt, H., A. Sanz, and D. Braun. 2009. Motive individuellen Wahlverhaltens in Nebenwahlen: Eine theoretische Rekonstruktion und empirische Überprüfung. In: *Wahlen and Wähler. Analysen aus Anlass der Bundestagswahl 2005*, eds. O.W. Gabriel, B. Weßels, and J.W. Falter, 585–605. Wiesbaden: VS Verlag.

Van der Eijk, C., and H. Schmitt. 2009. Legitimacy and electoral abstentions in European Parliament elections. In *The legitimacy of the European Union after enlargement*, ed. Jacques Thomassen, 208–24. Oxford: Oxford University Press.

Attitudes to European Integration: Investigating East–West Heterogeneity

JOHN GARRY* & JAMES TILLEY**

*School of Politics, International Studies and Philosophy, Queen's University Belfast, Northern Ireland, UK; **Department of Politics and International Relations, University of Oxford, UK

ABSTRACT   The study of citizens' attitudes to the EU is in danger of splintering, with context-specific transition-based models being applied in the former communist countries, models that — at face value — have no applicability in the Western states. Using data from the 2004 European Election Study, we test a model of attitude generation that is applicable to the universe of member states but which allows for the strength of attitude determinants to vary across the Eastern and Western contexts. Based on the literature, we suspect that the economic and democratic aspects of the 'transition' in eastern Europe will be particularly important in shaping views on the EU in that context. Specifically, we test the following hypotheses: (1) positive retrospective economic evaluations are a stronger determinant of support for integration in the East than in the West, and (2) a positive evaluation of EU democracy relative to one's own country's democracy is a stronger determinant of support for integration in the East than in the West. We find strong support for the first hypothesis, but no support for the second.

Introduction

There have now been a number of large-scale systematic studies of the determinants of the EU attitudes of citizens in former communist countries (Cichowski 2000; Tucker, Pacek, and Berinsky 2002; Caplanova, Marta, and

Correspondence Address: John Garry, School of Politics, International Studies and Philosophy, Queen's University Belfast, 21 University Square, Belfast BT7 1PA, Northern Ireland, UK. Email: j.garry@qub.ac.uk

Hudson 2004; Tverdova and Anderson 2004; Christin 2005; Elgün and Tillman 2007). These add to a large literature on the attitude determinants of citizens in Western states (for recent reviews see Hooghe and Marks 2005; McLaren 2006). However, to date there has not been a pan-European study incorporating both the Western and Eastern member states which assesses the relative importance of attitude determinants in these two contexts. In fact, the literature on attitude generation is in danger of splintering as context-specific models are applied in the East, models that — at face value — have no applicability in the West. Specifically, the 'Eastern' studies are typically based, in large part, on the impact of the transition from communism to post-communism. Citizens who have benefited from the transition to the free market and democracy are posited to support EU integration as this cements, and extends, the economic and democratic reforms. In Tucker, Pacek, and Berinsky's (2002) terms, transitional 'winners' will support the EU and transitional 'losers' will oppose it. While these transition-based models of EU attitudes are sensibly derived from the specific political and historical context of the former communist states, their very context specificity prohibits their application to the wider Europe. This is worrying from a general theoretical viewpoint as it renders impossible an explanation of attitude formation that can be elaborated for, and tested on, the single newly enlarged EU.

In order to avoid an East–West schism, we seek in this paper to incorporate into a single model both the Eastern and Western contexts while accommodating the possibility that certain determinants may have a much more powerful effect in one context than the other. Specifically, we *generalize* the factors that underlie the transition model, apply these to the universe of member states and test the possibility that these factors are indeed more important in the East than in the West. We begin by focusing on citizens' evaluations of recent economic performance. Given the link in the former communist states between attitudes to post-transition economic reform and attitudes to EU integration (Tucker, Pacek, and Berinsky 2002), we argue that retrospective economic evaluations will be a stronger predictor of EU attitudes in the East than the West. Next, we focus on the issue of democratization and argue that, given the recent democratic transition in former communist states, factors relating to democracy will be a stronger predictor of EU attitudes in the East than in the West. As was the case in the Mediterranean enlargement in the 1980s (when Greece, Portugal and Spain moved from recent authoritarian regimes into 'democratic' Europe), factors relating to democratic norms and institutions are likely to be particularly salient in the recently communist and authoritarian member states (Cichowski 2000).

East–West Heterogeneity

Two hypotheses about contextual determinants of attitudes to EU integration are derived from the unique nature of the transition of former communist states. The economic and democratic aspects of the transition suggest that factors relating to evaluations of democracy and (retrospective) evaluations of the economy in former communist states are particularly important drivers of attitudes to integration. Of course, a wide variety of other contextual factors could be important in the newly enlarged Europe in addition to the East versus West context that is studied in this paper. Given the dramatic nature of the 2004 enlargement, which incorporates a range of former communist states, it is the East–West distinction that is concentrated on here.

Economic Perceptions

Several analysts have argued that in former communist states the roots of contemporary attitudes to the EU lie in perceptions of the transition from communism to post-communism. The free market reforms of the post-Soviet era brought Eastern European states out of command-style economies towards much more liberal economic regimes. This economic transition benefited some citizens, but not others. Those who benefited from the free market reforms are keen to see such reforms buttressed and bedded down as much as possible so that they can retain their advantageous economic position. These citizens, who are 'winners' from the free market reform process, see European integration as a mechanism for cementing, and extending, the move to free markets. These 'winners' thus support European integration. In contrast, other citizens did poorly from the transition from a command economy to the free market and are thus sceptical of any moves to underpin or extend the market liberalization process. As Cichowshi (2000, 1248) states: 'Given what we know about those most "hurt" by market reforms (labour, pensioners, farmers), the EU does not offer them a quick resolution to their economic hardships ... European integration stands as the further institutionalisation of free market reforms, a prospect not necessarily welcomed by these individuals'.

Cichowski (2000) uses citizens' subjective perceptions of economic wellbeing to operationalize the notion of some people benefiting and others not benefiting from the free market reforms and finds support for the hypothesis that those with positive economic perceptions are likely to support the EU: 'They view integration as an extension of the positive benefits they have so far received from the liberalisation and transformation of their national economies. Thus, these attitudes regarding economic well-being may become a basis for individual attitudes about European integration' (*ibid.*, 1257).

Tucker, Pacek, and Berinsky (2002, 557) elaborate a similar argument and present a model that is 'designed explicitly for post communist countries'. They argue that 'membership of the EU can function as an implicit guarantee that the economic reforms undertaken since the end of communism will not be reversed' (*ibid.*, 557)[1] and that those who have benefited from transition ('winners') will be more likely to be supportive than those who did not benefit ('losers'). Like Cichowski, Tucker, Pacek, and Berinsky use economic perceptions to operationalize 'winners' and 'losers'. Using evidence from ten Central and Eastern European states, they (*ibid.*, 569) conclude that their results:

> ... provide strong evidence that the extent of support for membership in the European Union among post-Communist citizens is in large part a

function of the effects of the economic transition during the previous decade. Those who have benefited — as well as those who have lost — form opinions in a manner that is consistent with our theoretical proposition that citizens in transition countries view EU membership as a continuation of free market reforms, and thus support or oppose membership accordingly.

Christin (2005) also confirms this relationship, again using citizens' economic perceptions as the explanatory variable and drawing on data from twenty-one former communist states.[2] These various analyses emphasize the importance of the particular context of former communist countries and the role played by the transition to the free market in shaping EU views. Tucker, Pacek, and Berinsky (2002, 784) are particularly explicit in arguing that the former communist countries should be seen as a unique case due to their experience of transition to the free market. They state that 'there is no West European equivalent to the enormous social and economic shifts underway across the former communist world, and thus no equivalent to their effects on citizens as well'.

We argue that analysts of former communist states are right to emphasize the particularities of the post-communist case. However, rather than seeing the case as unique and non-comparable, we seek to incorporate its particularities into a single pan-European model. We argue that this is relatively easy to accomplish by modelling the effects of economic perceptions on attitudes to integration in both the West[3] and East while explicitly allowing, following the above authors, the effects to be much stronger in the East than in the West. Thus, we have two aims. First, we wish to establish whether the retrospective economic evaluations model predicts attitudes to European integration in the East as well as in the West. Secondly, we wish to test whether the strength of the effect varies across East and West. Specifically, we test the following hypothesis.

H1:   Positive retrospective economic evaluations are a stronger predictor of pro-integration views in former communist countries than in Western states.

Democracy

In addition to free market reform the other key aspect of the post-communist transition relates to democratic reforms and to the emerging democratic institutions of these states as they break from their authoritarian past. Just as opinion is divided on economic reforms, there is no consensus on the democratic reforms, with some citizens much more in favour than others. Cichowski (2000, 1249), for example, emphasizes both the democratic as well as economic aspects of EU integration in former communist states:

In the Central and Eastern European context, not only is EU membership viewed in terms of economic living standard increases, but it also means strengthening the institutional base for democracy and capitalism. The consolidation of democratic institutions is as much an interest to these citizens as personal economic benefit ... Wider European unity is conceptualised in terms of stabilising democratic norms as they develop in the post communist societies of Central and Eastern Europe.

Cichowski (2000) argues that the enlargement to incorporate former communist states is similar to the enlargement that incorporated Greece, Portugal and Spain. Economic factors were certainly important for the Mediterranean enlargement but these three states were also newly democratizing states whose applications for membership were in significant part driven by the desire to bed down democratic political institutions and lessen the possibility of any reversion to authoritarian rule. The desire for EU membership as a mechanism for consolidating domestic democratic institutions was a key feature of debates at this second stage of enlargement of the EU (Tsoukalis 1981). It would be unsurprising if factors relating to democracy were also highly salient in the recent enlargement involving former communist states. As Cichowski (2000, 1250) states: 'We might expect Central and Eastern European citizens to link accession to the continuation and permanence of their new democracies. European integration becomes the bridge to democratic dreams as symbolised by the West'. Citizens who are keen to cement and extend democratic reform and decrease the chances of reversion to authoritarian rule might be expected to strongly favour EU integration as a mechanism facilitating this, given that the EU 'locks in' member states into democratic norms and procedures (Moravcsik and Vachudova 2003). On the other hand, citizens in former communist states who are unimpressed with, and feel they have not benefited from, democratic reforms may be much less supportive of the idea of European integration.

Issues relating to democracy are also relevant for citizens in Western states. Rohrschneider (2002) argues that for citizens who feel unrepresented by EU institutions their support for the EU and EU integration is reduced and that this is particularly so in states with relatively high quality national democratic institutions. Similarly, Sanchez-Cuena (2000, 169) analysed Western states and found that 'the worse citizens' opinion of national institutions and the better their opinion of supranational ones, the stronger their support for European integration'. This line of argument draws on the work of Anderson (1998), who emphasized the role of national domestic conditions (including satisfaction with democracy and democratic institutions) in determining attitudes towards EU integration. Our argument here is that, given the key significance of democratic factors in the transition from communism to post-communism, we expect attitudes to democracy will play a more important role in shaping EU attitudes in the East than in the West. We emphasize that we expect attitudes to democracy to be linked to EU attitudes in both the West and the East, but given the democratizing context of the former communist states, this link will be particularly strong in Eastern states.[4]

H2:   Positive views of EU democracy relative to domestic democracy
are a stronger predictor of pro-integration views in the East than
in the West.

Data and Methods

We use the European Election Study (EES) 2004 pooled dataset, which
contains responses to a core set of questions from representative samples of
twenty-four of the twenty-five EU member states. These surveys were
conducted shortly after the European Parliament elections of June 2004
across the twenty-four countries included.[5] Due to missing measures of the
dependent and independent variables, we do not include Lithuania in our
final analyses, limiting our total number of country cases to twenty-three. As
we are interested in predicting attitudes to European integration, our dependent variable is a measure of support for further integration. Although
previous studies (for example, Gabel and Palmer 1995; Gabel 1998; Hooghe
and Marks 2004, 2005; McLaren 2004) have generated a scale of attitudes
to the EU by summing together responses to a number of questions regarding membership and integration, we are in the position of being able to use
a single item ten-point scale that directly captures attitudes to European
integration. An advantage of such a scale is that it renders the results of the
analysis more readily interpretable than results generated using a summed
scale, because the scale (that we use) is qualitatively anchored. The wording
is as follows:

> Some say European unification should be pushed further. Others say it
> already has gone too far. What is your opinion? Please indicate your
> views using a 10-point-scale. On this scale, 1 means unification 'has
> already gone too far' and 10 means it 'should be pushed further'. What
> number on this scale best describes your position?

Economic perceptions were measured with the standard retrospective
sociotropic question as below:

> Compared to 12 months ago, do you think that the general economic
> situation in [your country] is: a) A lot better; b) A little better; c) Stayed
> the same; d) A little worse; e) A lot worse?

This was recoded and reversed, with –2 representing 'a lot worse' and 2
representing 'a lot better'.[6] We also create a measure of satisfaction with
EU democracy. As we want this to be relative to satisfaction in the
national democratic system — given that, following the earlier discussion,
it is likely to be the perceived inferiority (or superiority) of the EU institutions to national institutions that generates opposition (or support) — we
combine two items that ask about democratic satisfaction. These read as
follows:

On the whole, how satisfied are you with the way democracy works in [your country]? Are you: a) Very satisfied; b) Fairly satisfied; c) Not very satisfied; d) Not at all satisfied.

All in all again, are you very satisfied, fairly satisfied, not very satisfied or not at all satisfied with the way democracy works in the European Union? Are you: a) Very satisfied; b) Fairly satisfied; c) Not very satisfied; d) Not at all satisfied.

These items were recoded and reversed, with 4 representing 'very satisfied' and 1 representing 'not at all satisfied' for each question. We then generated a measure of relative satisfaction with the EU by subtracting the score on the national democracy question from the EU democracy question. This gives a −3 to +3 scale, where 3 indicates more satisfaction with EU democracy and −3 more satisfaction with national democracy.

At the country level, of course, we are interested in the post-communist status of the country and we include a dummy variable scored 1 for the post-communist states (in our dataset: the Czech Republic, Estonia, Hungary, Latvia, Poland, Slovakia and Slovenia), and 0 for the other EU members (in our dataset: Austria, Belgium, Britain, Cyprus,[7] Denmark, Finland, France, Germany, Greece, Ireland, Italy, Luxembourg, the Netherlands, Portugal and Spain).

Additionally, we include a range of control variables in our model. At the individual level, these are socio-structural characteristics that have been found to be predictive of attitudes towards EU integration in the past. These are age, sex, social class,[8] years of education[9] and public sector employment. At the country level we also include a measure of how well each country fares in terms of financial benefits from the EU. This is now well established as a good predictor of EU support at the country level (Anderson and Reichert 1996; Diez Medrano 2003; Brinegar, Jolly, and Kitschelt 2004) and is, of course, correlated with post-communist status (all the post-communist countries are net beneficiaries of the EU budget). We operationalize this as percentage of gross national income that countries receive as net EU transfers; this varies in 2004 from positive transfers of 2.52 per cent in Greece to negative transfers of 0.44 per cent in the Netherlands.[10]

As discussed, although our dependent variable is measured at the individual level, we have independent variables at the individual and country level. Moreover we are especially interested in interactions between these two levels; our hypotheses relate to differences in how individual attitudes affect individuals' positions on integration according to post-communist status. Given this, we specify a series of hierarchical models by introducing random intercept coefficients. This explicitly takes account of the two-level (country and individual) nature of the data. This kind of model corrects for the dependence of observations within countries (intra-class correlation) and makes adjustments to both within and between parameter estimates for the clustered nature of the data (Snijders and Bosker 1999). As we have an interval level-dependent variable (1–10 scale), we estimate a hierarchical generalized linear model, with a Gaussian link function. We have used a maximum likelihood estimation procedure.

Results

Before turning to the table showing the regression models, it is worth examining the raw country-level differences. Figure 1 shows mean levels of support for further integration by country, with countries in order of EU entry. There are two clear patterns: first, people in the post-communist countries are more supportive of the EU than people in other countries, scoring almost half a point higher on the scale on average; and, secondly, people in countries that are large net beneficiaries of EU transfers (the post-communist countries, together with Greece, Portugal, Spain and Cyprus) are generally more supportive than citizens living elsewhere. These large differences by country also disguise quite large differences within countries. The standard deviation of our scale for the total sample is 2.7, and in no country does this fall below 2.2. In the regression models we present here, we thus attempt to explain some of these country-level differences, some of the individual-level

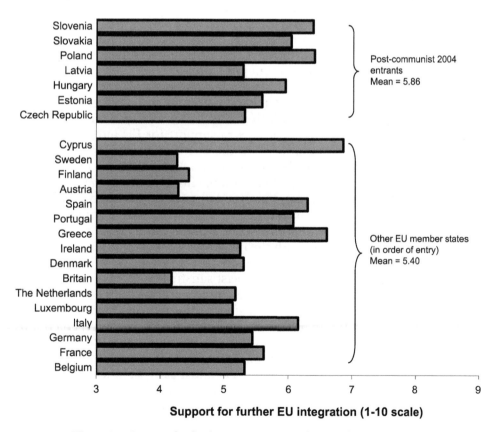

Figure 1. Support for further EU integration by member state, 2004.

differences, but, most importantly, whether the explanations for the latter are the same for all countries. In particular, do the decision-making mechanisms that citizens rely on when generating their views about integration vary according to whether citizens reside in post-communist states or established member states?

In Table 1 we report the results of four multi-level linear regression models. The first of these models simply includes our individual-level control variables and a dummy variable for post-communist country status, the second adds another country-level variable of fiscal transfer, the third includes our key individual-level variables of satisfaction with EU democracy and retrospective economic perceptions and, finally, the fourth model directly tests our two hypotheses by interacting democracy satisfaction and economic perceptions with post-communist status.

Taking model 1 first, we see that standard predictors of support for integration behave as we would expect. In terms of our control variables, support for further integration is associated with being: relatively highly educated, middle class, a public sector worker and male. The effect of post-communist status is also quite large and statistically significant at the 10 per cent level. Controlling for individual-level socio-economic characteristics actually slightly increases the gap between post-communist and other states to over half a point on our 1–10 scale. As model 2 shows, this gap is at least partially due to the higher rates of transfers that post-communist countries receive, as the effect of fiscal transfers is statistically significant and slightly reduces the coefficient of post-communist status.

More interestingly, as model 3 shows, our measures of economic perceptions and satisfaction with EU democracy are not just strongly related to support for integration — though they are — but also account for a large degree of post-communist countries' extra support for EU integration. This is largely due to the fact that citizens of the post-communist states are more positive on average about EU democracy than national democracy, whereas citizens of other EU states prefer their national institutions. None the less the most striking features of model 3 are the large effects of our two key variables of economic perceptions and democracy satisfaction. People with the most positive economic perceptions score around half a standard deviation more on our scale than those with the most negative perceptions, and people that are the most satisfied with EU democracy score nearly a full standard deviation higher on our scale than the least satisfied.

But what of the hypothesized greater impact of both of these effects in the post-communist states? The inclusion of the two interaction terms in model 4 means that the main effects in Table 1 of economic perceptions and satisfaction with EU democracy are the effects for the West, with the effects in the East the combination of the main coefficient with the interaction coefficient. As can be seen, there is a statistically significant difference in how economic perceptions affect citizens in the East and West. In fact, the effect of economic perceptions in post-communist countries is also 50 per cent higher than in the Western countries, which provides strong support for our first hypothesis. Our second hypothesis, by contrast, is

Table 1. Multi-level linear regression models predicting support for further European integration

	Model 1		Model 2		Model 3		Model 4	
	B	SE	B	SE	B	SE	B	SE
Age (divided by 100)	-0.18	0.12	-0.18	.12	-0.07	0.12	-0.06	0.12
Male	0.29***	0.04	0.29***	0.04	0.27***	0.04	0.27***	0.04
Upper middle class	0.66***	0.07	0.66***	0.07	0.57***	0.07	0.57***	0.07
Middle class	0.35***	0.05	0.35***	0.05	0.29***	0.05	0.29***	0.05
Lower middle class	0.15**	0.06	0.15**	0.06	0.11*	0.06	0.11*	0.06
Other	0.42***	0.12	0.42***	0.12	0.37***	0.12	0.38***	0.12
Working class	0.00	–	0.00	–	0.00	–	0.00	–
Years of education post-14	0.07***	0.01	0.07***	0.01	0.07***	0.01	0.07***	0.01
Public sector worker	0.09**	0.04	0.09**	0.04	0.10**	0.04	0.10**	0.04
Post-communist country	0.56*	0.33	0.44	0.27	0.25	0.30	0.29	0.30
Fiscal transfers (% of GNI 2004)			0.32**	0.16	0.25	0.15	0.24	0.16
Prefer democracy in European Parliament to National Parliament (–3 to 3)					0.40***	0.03	0.41***	0.03
Retrospective economic perceptions (–2 to 2)					0.34***	0.02	0.30***	0.02
Post-communist x democracy							-0.04	0.06
Post-communist x economic perceptions							0.13***	0.04
Intercept	4.67***	0.20	4.53***	0.20	4.79***	0.20	4.79***	0.20
Sigma u	0.72	0.10	0.66	0.10	0.65	0.10	0.65	0.10
Sigma e	2.59	0.01	2.59	0.01	2.56	0.01	2.56	0.01
Log likelihood	-44,953.6		-44,951.6		-44,700.0		-40,694.6	

*$p<0.10$, **$p<0.05$, ***$p<0.01$.
Country $n=23$, individua $n=18,930$.
Source: EES (2004).

completely unsupported; the interaction term is not statistically significant and satisfaction with EU democracy seems to have very similar effects in both groups of countries.

Discussion

Public opinion influences the development of the European Union, both in terms of determining the nature of the integration process and in providing political legitimacy for the project. As Gabel (1998, 333) states, the attitudes of EU citizens 'shape and constrain the process of European integration … [and] provide the political foundation for integration. Since EU law lacks a supranational means of enforcement, the endurance of the EU political system vitally depends on public compliance with and acceptance of EU law'. Given that the EU essentially depends, for its continued functioning, on an acceptable level of backing from the public, the important question arises: why do some members of the public support the integration process and others do not? This question has received a great deal of academic attention and many analysts have assessed the relative merits of different theories of attitude formation. The expansion of the EU to incorporate the former communist states of eastern Europe has obviously transformed the EU into a much more diverse political entity. This substantial enhancement of the heterogeneity of the EU may have a significant impact on the continued success (or otherwise) of extant theories that seek to explain EU citizens' attitudes to the EU.

Our analysis explored the possibility that the drivers of attitudes to EU integration may vary across the Western and Eastern contexts. In line with expectations regarding the specific nature of the post-communist context, economic evaluations emerged as a more powerful predictor of EU attitudes in the Eastern context than in the Western context. Yet, we should note that arguments regarding dissatisfaction with post-communist democratic institutions driving support for EU integration seem less well supported. Unsurprisingly, people generally are more supportive of integration when they prefer EU institutions to their own domestic institutions, but more surprisingly given the previous literature there appears no extra effect in the post-communist states. Although the post-communist institutions fare less well in comparison with the EU institutions than their Western counterparts, it is not the case that those in post-communist states rely on this judgement more heavily when evaluating arguments for integration. Overall, our findings highlight the need for explanations of EU attitude formation to be sensitive to context — not least the East–West context — and the need to incorporate possible context-based heterogeneity into our explanatory and modelling frameworks.

Notes

1. See also the discussion in Moravcsik and Vachudova (2003) about membership 'locking in' the former communist states into the EU and global economic order.

2. We should note that not all analysts rely on citizens' economic perceptions. For example, Caplanova, Marta, and Hudson (2004) use socio-demographic proxies such as education and income, positing that higher earners and the higher educated will have benefited more from free market reforms and will thus tend to be supportive of EU integration. None the less the standard operationalization is through economic perceptions.

3. See, for example, Gabel (1998), Gabel and Whitten (1997) Anderson and Reichart (1996).

4. It should be emphasized that our analysis does not exhaust the range of possible East–West differences in attitude formation. Most notably, we have not directly addressed — due to data limitations — the argument of Rohrschneider and Whitefield (2006) that the impact of political values and ideology on attitudes to EU integration may vary in strength across the eastern and western contexts. We plan to address this explicitly in future work.

5. Full details of the surveys are available at www.europeanelectionstudies.net.

6. Some authors have used prospective rather than retrospective economic perceptions (Hooghe and Marks 2004, 2005). It is retrospective evaluations that are more theoretically relevant here, however.

7. Cyprus and Malta also joined the EU in 2004 together with the eight post-communist states. Malta is not in our dataset unfortunately, but it is worth noting that the inclusion or exclusion of Cyprus as part of the 'Western' group of countries makes no substantive difference to our results.

8. The class measure is based on self-reported perceived social class, rather than occupational status. The full question asks people to place themselves into one of the following categories: working class, lower middle class, middle class, upper middle class, upper class, or other. We have combined the fourth and fifth categories to give a five-category variable, with working class as the reference category.

9. This measures years of full-time education after age fourteen. This means respondents that stated they finished education up to fourteen are coded as 0. All education-finishing ages after age twenty-five are combined, meaning the variable runs from 0 to 11.

10. These transfer figures are from the European Commission (2006) and include a simple adjustment for administrative expenditure in Belgium and Luxembourg. For these two countries we include the average of payments with and without administrative expenditure, without this adjustment Luxembourg appears to be a net contributor despite being the highest recipient once administrative expenditure is included. These adjustments do not affect our main substantive conclusions, but we think it is the most appropriate way of dealing with administrative expenditure.

References

Anderson, C. 1998. When in doubt, use proxies: attitudes toward domestic politics and support for European integration. *Comparative Political Studies* 31: 569–601.

Anderson, C.J., and M.S. Reichert. 1996. Economic benefits and support for membership in the EU: A cross-national analysis. *Journal of Public Policy* 15: 231–49.

Brinegar, A., S. Jolly, and H. Kitschelt. 2004. Varieties of capitalism and political divides over European integration. In *European integration and political conflict,* eds. G. Marks and M. Steenbergen, 62–92. New York: Cambridge Univ. Press.

Caplanova, A., O. Marta, and J. Hudson. 2004. Eastern European attitudes to integration with Western Europe. *Journal of Common Market Studies* 42, no. 2: 271–88.

Christin, T. 2005. Economic and political basis of attitudes towards the EU in Central and East European countries in the 1990s. *European Union Politics* 6, no. 1: 29–57.

Cichowski, R.A. 2000. Western dreams, Eastern realities: Support for the European Union in Central and Eastern Europe. *Comparative Political Studies* 33, no. 10: 1243–78.

Diez Medrano, J. 2003. *Framing Europe: Attitudes to European integration in Germany, Spain, and the United Kingdom.* Princeton, NJ: Princeton Univ. Press.

Elgün, O., and E. Tillman. 2007. Exposure to European Union policies and support for membership in the candidate countries. *Political Research Quarterly* 60, no. 3: 391–400.

European Commission. 2006. Allocation of 2005 EU expenditure by member state, http://ec.europa.eu/budget/documents/revenue_expenditure_en.html.

Gabel, M. 1998. Public support for European integration: An empirical test of five theories. *Journal of Politics* 60, no. 2: 333–54.

Gabel, M., and H. Palmer. 1995. Understanding variation in public support for European integration. *European Journal of Political Research* 27: 3–19.

Gabel, M., and G. Whitten. 1997. Economic conditions, economic perceptions and public support for European integration. *Political Behaviour* 19, no. 1: 81–96.

Hooghe, L., and G. Marks. 2004. Does identity or economic rationality drive public opinion on European integration?. *PS: Political Science and Politics* 37: 415–20.

Hooghe, L., and G. Marks. 2005. Calculation, community, and cues: Public opinion on European integration. *European Union Politics* 6, no. 4: 419–43.

McLaren, Lauren. 2004. Opposition to European integration and fear of loss of national identity: Debunking a basic assumption regarding hostility to the integration project. *European Journal of Political Research* 43: 895–911.

McLaren, Lauren. 2006. *Identity, interests and attitudes to European integration.* New York: Palgrave.

Moravcsik, A., and M.A. Vachudova. 2003. National interests, state power, and EU enlargement. *East European Politics and Societies* 17, no. 1: 42–57.

Rohrschneider, R. 2002. The democracy deficit and mass support for an EU-wide government. *American Journal of Political Science* 46, no. 2: 463–75.

Rohrschneider, R., and S. Whitefield. 2006. Political parties, public opinion and European integration in post-communist countries. *European Union Politics* 7, no. 1: 141–60.

Sanchez-Cuena, I. 2000. The political basis of support for European integration. *European Union Politics* 1, no. 2: 147–71.

Snijders, T., and R. Bosker. 1999. *Multilevel analysis: An introduction to basic and advanced multilevel modeling.* Trowbridge: The Cromwell Press.

Tsoukalis, L. 1981. *The European Community and its Mediterranean enlargement.* Sydney, Australia: Allen and Unwin.

Tucker, J.A., A.C. Pacek, and A.J. Berinsky. 2002. Transitional winners and losers: Attitudes toward EU membership in post-communist countries. *American Journal of Political Science* 46, no. 3: 557–71.

Tverdova, Y., and C. Anderson. 2004. Choosing the West? Referendum choices on EU membership in East-Central Europe. *Electoral Studies* 23: 185–208.

Dynamics in European Political Identity

ANGELIKA SCHEUER* & HERMANN SCHMITT**

*GESIS — Leibniz Institute for the Social Sciences, Mannheim, Germany; **MZES,
University of Mannheim, Mannheim, Germany

ABSTRACT   The creation of a political community is a difficult yet vital task for the
European Union. Using Eurobarometer time series of 25 years and the European Election Study of 2004, this article reviews the state of the development of a 'sense of
community' with regard to two concepts: Identity is measured in terms of perceived citizenship and pride to be a European citizen; we-feeling is captured by assessing trust in
European people and acceptance of new member countries. A collective identity is
growing slowly among the European citizens, but the data suggest a center–periphery
distinction between the core members and the joiners of the different enlargement
waves. EU citizens trust each other, but the East–West continental divide still remains
detectable.

Introduction

The existence of a collective identity is generally seen as one of the central
preconditions for EU democracy (e.g. Scharpf 1999). A collective political
identity constitutes a political community. The idea of a political community,
in turn, is intimately linked with the concept of citizenship. The creation of
a citizenry, i.e. the codification of the rights and duties of individual citizens,
was a core element of the process of nation-building (Kuhnle 1993). This citizenry, at the same time, is the source of authority of any democratic government: the principle of democracy requires that powers and executive
competencies must originate in and be justified by the citizens subjected to
them. The aim of our enquiries is, therefore, to ascertain if the citizens of the

Correspondence Address: Angelika Scheuer, GESIS — Leibniz Institute for the Social Sciences,
P.O. Box 122155, D-68072 Mannheim, Germany. E-mail: angelika.scheuer@gesis.org

European Union share a common political identity and, if they do, what have the recent waves of enlargement of the EU done to it?[1]

European integration started out as an alliance of nation-states. It concerned first and foremost economic issues. Economic integration reached a peak with the realization of the Single European Market when member states transferred important policy-making competencies to the European Community. The Maastricht Treaty, which codifies this transfer of competencies, is actually said to have shifted the balance of EU government from a formerly predominantly intergovernmental to a now mainly supranational mode. In policy areas where intergovernmental decision making was replaced by supranational decision making, the position of the European Parliament as the representative body of EU citizens has been strengthened.

The increasing role of supranational, as opposed to intergovernmental, decision making and the establishment of a European citizenship might have promoted the development of a political community of the EU. But the growing-together of a political community depends at least as much on people's self-perceptions and identifications as on the provision of rights of citizenship or on predominant modes of government. Therefore, our central question can be reformulated as follows: do EU citizens identify themselves as such? Do they perceive their fellow EU citizens to be alike? Have European citizens developed a 'sense of community' that unites old and new members?

Historical Sources of Unity and Diversity

History has shown that the emergence of a sense of belonging and community and related attitudes, such as perceptions of identity and solidarity, takes a long time. Compared to the time that nation-states took to consolidate, the history of European integration is still rather short. Feelings of identity and solidarity can hardly have fully developed during these brief periods of history. But, of course, centuries of common European history elapsed before European integration began. The discourse dedicated to construct a European unity and identity makes reference to common roots in history, religion, science and culture in order to emphasize Europe as a distinctive cultural entity. 'Graeco-Roman civilization, Christianity, and the ideas of Enlightenment, Science, Reason, Progress and Democracy are declared the core elements of this European legacy' (Stråth 2002, 388).

The tradition of the Greek *polis* and the Roman Empire influenced in similar ways the development of institutions in the legal system, the armed forces and the administration of European nation-states. All over Europe, the same sequence of reference cultures came into force: first Greek and Roman, then (during the Renaissance) Italian, and German and Austrian during the Enlightenment and Romanticism. Likewise, Europeans used to refer to common cultural achievements (literature, music, architecture) and to common European symbols: Roman monuments, the victory over Islam, the Crusades, the French Revolution (Pfetsch 1997, 104–5). Last, but not least, Europeans consider themselves to be a community of values and ideas. The idea of liberty, of democracy, of the modern nation-state, individualism, human rights, freedom of speech, rationality, the political republic, and the separation of Church and State — all this is considered to be genuinely 'European' (Mintzel 1997, 325–6).

Europe is characterized not only by its common heritage. There is as much diversity and conflict as there are common roots. Religious and linguistic differences essentially underlie the major ethnic cleavages that have regularly been the reason for confrontation and war. Three religious cleavages are at the basis of distinct socio-cultural areas on the European continent: the division between Latin and Orthodox Christianity, that between the Christian and the Islamic world and, finally, the division between Catholics and Protestants. In addition, Europe exhibits a great variety of languages, which has become even more distinctive with the development of the nation-states in the nineteenth century. It is against this background that some think of Europe as a huge 'multicultural society' composed of a variety of religious, national and regional cultures (Mintzel 1997, 332–6).

A European Political Community?

The history of Europe suggests that the traditions of diversity, division and conflict are at least as strong as the common cultural heritage. This history of diversity does not necessarily prevent the evolution of a European political community. However, the sheer existence of nation-states based on a century of cultural and political autonomy constitutes an obvious obstacle. First, these nation-states are linguistic communities that guarantee the communicative competence of every citizen.[2] EU citizens, by contrast, are confronted with an immense linguistic variety. This apparent Babel make the development of a Europe-wide public more difficult, but not impossible — as we can see from the fact that European political communication is already taking place (i.e. de Vreese 2003; Koopmans and Erbe 2004). However, given the complex institutional structure of the EU, no effective system of opinion formation and interest intermediation has fully developed yet (e.g. Schmitt 2005). As a result, processes of legitimizing EU government still depend on the effectiveness of the respective national (sub-)systems. This might suggest that objective conditions for the genesis of a European political community are not very favourable, but such a development is not impossible on principle.

Other factors might have promoted the development of a European political community. Not least among them is the obvious economic success of the process of European integration (Dalton and Eichenberg 1992; Eichenberg and Dalton 1993). Also, the greater permeability of national borders after the agreement of Schengen, as well as the ever-increasing contact frequency of European citizens as a result of progressing economic integration, might have promoted perceptions of community and mutual solidarity among EU citizens (Schmitt and Treiber-Reif 1990; Bosch and Newton 1995). The political concept of a European identity was designed by the Copenhagen summit in December 1973 and followed by the establishment of symbols like the flag and the anthem in the beginning of the 1980s. The common currency is the strongest symbol of European unity because it comes closest to citizens' everyday life (Risse 2003). In the same way, the introduction of European citizenship is a symbol that imitates the nation-state in order to stimulate a European political community.

Our prime purpose is to determine the degree to which the EU has developed into a political community. After this brief review of objective conditions, we will now turn to both a more subjective and empirical view. According to Easton (1965, 177), a political community exists when members show some readiness or ability to work together to resolve their political problems. That a European political community in such terms exists is unquestioned, but we are interested in knowing whether European citizens, during almost half a century of European integration, have developed a European 'sense of community'. The existence of a political community does not necessarily require that its members are aware of it — i.e. the prior existence of a sense of community. However, the stronger such a sense of community is developed, the greater are the system's stress-reducing capabilities (Lindberg and Scheingold 1970).

This concept *sense of community* was first introduced by Karl Deutsch. He defines it as 'a matter of mutual sympathy and loyalties; of "we-feeling", trust and mutual consideration; of partial identification in terms of self-images and interests; of mutually successful predictions of behaviour, and of co-operative action in accordance with it' (Deutsch et al. 1957, 36). Easton (1975) follows Deutsch in his conceptualization of the 'sense of *social* community'; in his view, cohesion emerges between people regardless of the type of political regime in which they live. He, therefore, distinguishes this 'sense of *social* community' from a more specific 'sense of *political* community'. In his typology of political support, the latter represents the highest (i.e. the most basic and enduring) category of diffuse support for the political system.

Our empirical investigation of the sense of a European community distinguishes two basic dimensions. *Identification* refers to the citizens themselves: do they consider themselves as European citizens and are they proud to be European? *We-feeling* refers to fellow citizens: do European citizens consider their fellow Europeans to be as trustworthy as their countrymen? Which new members, if any, are they ready to accept into 'their' Union? Figure 1 illustrates this conceptualization and specifies the operationalization strategy pursued in the following.

These notions of *identification* and *we-feeling* are compatible with modern theories of intergroup relations. Their starting point is the distinction between ingroups and outgroups (Tajfel and Turner 1986). Minimal differentiation is sufficient to give rise to an ingroup–outgroup distinction. This is reinforced by overstating similarity within the group and differences to other groups. Ingroup membership is an important factor in the formation of personal identity. Ingroup–outgroup relations are driven by social processes of categorization, comparison, competition and conflict. As a result of these dynamics, perceptions of ingroups are biased toward homogeneity, and the attitudes towards outgroups and their members are

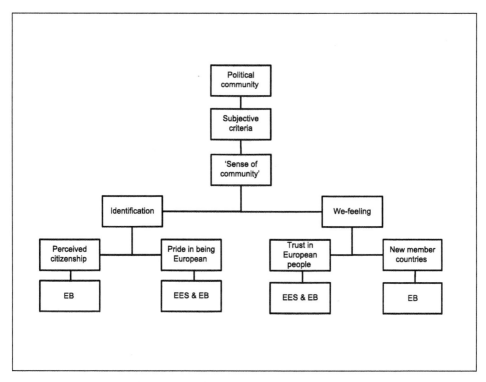

Figure 1.   Concepts, indicators and data sources. EES, European Election Study 2004; EB, Eurobarometer.

characterized by stereotyping and hostility. In this view, the evolution of a sense of community among EU citizens is the result of ingroup formation. Shortly after World War II, intergroup conflict between European societies was still extremely high. One of the central aims of the founding fathers of the European Union was to reduce conflict and overcome hostility between European societies by creating a new, superior ingroup which eventually would lead to the development of European identifications and we-feelings. We aim at measuring the success of European ingroup formation after half a century of economic and political integration, and after five successive waves of enlargement. The data that are used for this purpose are from the European Election Study 2004 (EES) plus selected Eurobarometer trends (EB). The indicators are discussed one by one, in the sequence suggested by the analytical scheme above.

Identifications

This section is dedicated to monitoring the evolution of European identifications. First, mass perceptions of European citizenship are tracked over a period of twenty-five years (1982 to 2007). Secondly, the development of pride in being European is compared across countries.

Perceived citizenship

Eurobarometer have used two different instruments for the analysis of European identification. The first was fielded eleven times between 1982 and 1992, and now repeated in the European Election Study 2004. This question asks whether people, in addition to their national citizenship, also consider themselves as European citizens.[3] The second instrument started a new Eurobarometer time series in 1992 when the first trend was discontinued. In twenty surveys between 1992 and 2007, people were asked to think about their future political identification.[4] Although the two measures are not strictly comparable, they still offer an impression of the direction of trends over the whole period. Detailed results for the more recent trend are documented in Table A1; these figures report, country by country, proportions of respondents who think of themselves as European citizens.

Here, we concentrate on describing the overall trends using both indicators (Figure 2). The lines report proportions of respondents who 'never' think of themselves as European citizens (according to the first indicator), and who see themselves in the near future as 'only national' (according to the second). Choosing these negative poles seems to be the best way to make the two trends comparable. Average proportions are displayed for six country groups: the original six plus the countries of the five successive expansions. This presentation of the data follows the expectation that duration of membership has a positive impact on identification levels: the longer the country is a member of the EU, the stronger should be European identification and the weaker national-only identification. We thus expect to find a pattern similar to the one identified for the development of general EU support (see, e.g., Schmitt and Treiber-Reif 1990; Dalton and Eichenberg 1992; Eichenberg and Dalton 1993; Bosch and Newton 1995). This expectation, however, is not fully borne out by the data. Rather, country group characteristics come to the fore. While citizens in the original six member countries are still the most 'European' (i.e. the less exclusively national), the first and oldest expansion (adding the UK, Ireland and Denmark to the Community) brought in more Euro-distant publics. Contrary to this, the second expansion (adding Spain, Portugal and Greece) integrated distinctly pro-European publics; these citizens consider themselves as 'European' as those in the founding member countries. The third expansion of the Union (adding Austria, Sweden and Finland) is somewhere in between: fewer 'European self-perceptions' than in southern Europe, but more than in Britain, Ireland and Denmark, and the trend displays an increasing degree of European identification. The latest and largest expansions of the Union — adding eight post-communist countries of central and eastern Europe plus Cyprus and Malta in 2004 as well as Bulgaria and Romania in 2007 — brought in surprisingly European-minded citizens: One in two citizens of the youngest member countries thinks of herself as a European citizen. However, only the longer trends will show how identification is developing in these new member countries.

The duration argument also implies that European identifications should grow more or less steadily over time, while national-only identifications

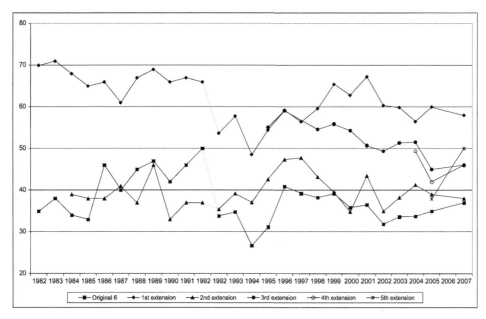

Figure 2. Feeling like a European citizen, 1982–1992 (percentage 'never'), and thinking of oneself as European or national, 1992–2007 (percentage 'only national'). *Source*: Eurobarometer surveys 1982–2007, weighted data.

should decrease. This expectation is again not fully in accordance with empirical evidence. The general pattern is not one of linear trends. Rather, we observe fluctuations that affect the different publics in more or less the same way. Tentative explanations for these ups and downs refer to two factors: first, changes in basic economic conditions, social welfare cutbacks and security concerns (dissolution of the communist bloc and war in former Yugoslavia) and, secondly, the increasing importance of EU policy making for everyday life (Niedermayer 1997). In addition, in the early 1990s, the debate on European Monetary Union, in particular, may have depressed European identifications (Lilli 1998).

Pride in being European
Pride in being European is our second indicator of European identification.[5] When we test the dimensionality of European pride and self-perceptions as a European citizen, we find that both attitudes are indeed originating in the same latent attitudinal construct (Table A1). This is so everywhere, though in some countries somewhat more pronounced (e.g. in the Netherlands) than in others (e.g. in Greece). This is not to say that the two indicators are equally distributed if it comes to country patterns (Table 1). Other things being equal, southerners seem to be prouder than citizens in the northern member countries. To be sure, geographical locations are poor explainers of political attitudes. Whether this 'southern' pattern has to do with economic factors (the South is a major receiver of transfers from the structural fund) or with

Table 1.   Pride to be a citizen of the EU, 1995–2004

	EES 2004	Flash 1995	2004–1995
Luxembourg	76	70	6
Ireland	74	64	10
Portugal	74	64	10
Cyprus	74		
France	73	65	8
Spain	67	66	1
Italy	64	80	−16
Greece	61	47	14
Belgium	60	60	0
Hungary	52		
Germany	49	42	7
Poland	46		
Britain	43		
Denmark	43	49	−6
Slovenia	42		
Austria	40	46	−6
Slovakia	37		
Finland	37	41	−4
Northern Ireland	31		
Czech Republic	29		
The Netherlands	26	45	−19
Estonia	25		
Latvia	24		
Sweden	23	37	−14

Percentage 'very proud' or 'fairly proud'.
Source: European Election Study (EES) 2004 and Eurobarometer Flash 47 (1995), weighted data.

cultural factors ('Latin Europeans' are allegedly more expressive than others when it comes to emotions like pride) cannot be answered at this point, however. In addition to geography, duration of membership seems to matter somewhat more here, with citizens from younger non-southern member countries being less proud than others.

Looking at the dynamics, we see signs of a growing gap between proud and non-proud national publics over the last decade. In 2004, we find everything between three quarters and one quarter of our respondents being proud of their European citizenship, both in old and new member countries. Significant decreases are notable in the Netherlands (−19), Italy (−16) and Sweden (−14); the steepest increases are diagnosed for Greece (+14), Portugal (+10) and Ireland (+10). The corresponding shifts in perceived citizenship are much smaller. Assuming that we can exclude methods effects, pride in being European seems to include a much stronger evaluative component that reacts to current and concrete political events and decisions. The comparative stability of self-perception as European point to the fact that it can be considered an affective attitude (Scheuer 2005, 70f).

We-feelings

Our operational definition of 'sense of community' distinguishes two dimensions: identifications and we-feelings. We now turn to the second and investigate, first, whether EU citizens trust their fellow Europeans and, secondly, to what degree Europeans are ready to accept more member countries into the EU.

Trust in European people

Trust is a fundamental condition for the development of a sense of community. It is expected to increase with growing experiences of positive conduct of fellow citizens. So, here again, duration of membership should play an important role. Moreover, the existence of a common enemy is a potential factor contributing to the development of a sense of community. For most of the post-war period, the communist threat was an external reference point that might have fostered perceptions of a common bond amongst the people of the EU. Actually, since the collapse of the Soviet Empire, observers had been complaining about the return of nationalism, and fears had grown that the community may fall apart without the eastern threat. This did not happen, however, as we know by now. Rather, the EU was able to integrate a major part of the former communist bloc. How successful is this integration in terms of we-feelings can be seen from the figures on trust in European people.

Trust in people of various countries has been measured repeatedly in Eurobarometer surveys using a four-point scale between 1970 and 1994.[6] As the list of member and candidate countries became longer, another instrument with a dichotomous answering scale proved to be more suitable.[7] The European Election Study also used the dichotomous answer categories.[8] Earlier work has shown that trust between EU member countries is generally higher than between members and non-members, and that mutual trust between the EU member countries is growing over time (Niedermayer 1995). We use the data based on the dichotomous answering scale and analyse for every country how much its people are trusted by the peoples from the other member countries (Table 2).

In 2004, the people from all but one 'old' EU-15 member countries are trusted by a two-thirds majority of fellow Europeans. Only the British miss this threshold: they are down at 51 per cent and have actually lost fifteen percentage points of trust over the past decade.[9] Considering the fact that levels of trust are even more stable than levels of perceived citizenship, this is a major drop indeed. What could have caused such a dramatic downfall? The only likely reason we can think of is the role that the UK played and continues to play in the Iraq war. It seems that the close alliance of the British with the Americans in this case has severely damaged the trust of their fellow Europeans. Interestingly, the loss in trust in the Brits is complemented by a

Table 2. Trust in other European people, 1995–2004

	2004 EU-25	2004 EU-15	1995 EU-15	Diff. EU-15 2004–1995
Swedes	83[a]	86	84	2
Danish	79	82	81	1
Finns	79	81	81	1
Luxembourgers	78	82	84	−2
Dutch	78	81	80	1
Spaniards	77	80	71	9
Belgians	75	78	82	−4
Portuguese	73	76	68	9
Germans	71	73	65	8
Austrians	70	73	75	−1
French	67	70	63	7
Irish	66	73	71	1
Italians	66	68	61	7
Greeks	66	66	62	4
Maltese	59	61		
Hungarians	59	59	56	3
Czech	56	55	50	6
Estonians	51	53		
British	51	50	66	−15
Latvians	50	52		
Cypriots	50	48		
Lithuanians	49	50		
Poles	47	48	46	2
Slovenes	47	46		
Slovaks	46	44		
Bulgarian	35	35		
Romanian	28	29		
Turks	26	26		

Percentage 'tend to trust'.
[a]Read: In 2004, 83 per cent of all non-Swedish EU-25 citizens considered the Swedes to be trustworthy.
Source: Eurobarometer 45 (1995) and European Election Study (EES) 2004; weighted data. Note that this question was not asked in the Belgian, British, Lithuanian, Maltese and Swedish survey of the EES 2004.

strong decrease of British pride in being European. The gap between British and Europeans was thus a case of mutual refusal. If this discord has been alleviated in the meantime cannot be answered, because unfortunately the trust question in the Eurobarometer surveys was discontinued in 1997.

An additional major finding with regard to the levels of trust among EU citizens is that there are indeed three classes of countries: old members, new members, and (then and present) candidate countries, with old members enjoying highest trust, new members somewhat less trust, and candidate countries only little trust. With the exception of the case of Britain, these three classes are accurately sorted one after the other. We also note that it does not make much of a difference for the levels of trust whether we analyse opinions of citizens in the old EU-15 or include the samples from the new member countries.

Acceptance of new members

There is no indication that the European Union after the last enlargements has found its final configuration yet. There is still a large number of would-be members beyond those who already take part. It is conceivable that some of them will join the EU in the future. Croatia and Turkey are official accession countries. The Former Yugoslavian Republic of Macedonia (FYROM) has also obtained the status of an accession country, but negotiations have not begun yet. All remaining Balkan countries are potential applicants: Albania, Bosnia and Herzegovina, Montenegro, Serbia as well as Kosovo (as defined by the UN resolution). The EU has repeatedly reaffirmed at the highest level its commitment for eventual EU membership of the western Balkan countries, provided they fulfil the accession criteria. While we-feelings are expressed toward actual members, the readiness to accept new member countries is indicative of a mental map in the minds of the citizens that may include some countries and reject others. Such a mental map does not have to be stable over time but may react to changes in the respective countries and the relationship to them. How welcome are additional member countries to the citizens of the EU, and did these attitudes change over time? Table 3 displays the development of approval to the accession of potential members for the last decade separately for old and new member states.

The potential candidates presented to the respondents can be sorted in three groups.[10] The first group contains Norway and Switzerland, both of which have declined membership on the bases of referenda, as well as Iceland, which has not signalled interest in joining the EU until now. The second group consists of a number of post-communist eastern and south-eastern countries, such as the remaining parts of former Yugoslavia (Croatia, Bosnia and Herzegovina, Serbia, Montenegro, and FYROM) as well as Ukraine and Albania. Turkey, finally, represents the third group and the bridge to the Islamic world.

The accession of Switzerland, Norway and Iceland receives strongest support, although their accession is currently just a hypothetical case. Being rich Western countries, their entry would not imply new burdens to the union but enlarge the group of net-payer countries. Old and new members welcome them alike, with roughly four out of five respondents saying they would be in favour of these countries becoming part of the EU in the future. The accession of the western Balkan countries is approved by less than a majority of the EU citizens. Among them, Croatia performs best (even better than Bulgaria and Romania before their accession), and Albania receives the least approval. The support for Croatia has increased strongly from about 30 per cent in the year 2000 to about 50 per cent in 2008, while the entry of Bulgaria and Romania was approved by only about 40 per cent

Table 3. Citizens' views about accession of new member countries, 1997–2008

	1997	1998	1999	2000	2001	2002	2005	2006	2008
EU-15									
Switzerland			70	70	75	75	76	77	77
Norway			71	70	74	75	76	76	78
Iceland					60	61	67	67	70
Romania	33	37	34	33	36	35	41	38	
Bulgaria	36	39	36	35	38	39	45	42	
Bosnia and Herzegovina				27	30	31	39	36	39
Croatia				31	33	35	47	46	51
FYROM				27	29	30	39	37	39
Yugoslavia[a]				29	32		36		
Serbia								34	36
Montenegro								37	39
Kosovo									33
Albania					27	27	32	30	33
Ukraine							38	37	42
Turkey			30	30	34	32	29	26	30
NMS-10									
Switzerland							83	87	85
Norway							82	86	84
Iceland							72	78	77
Romania							53	55	
Bulgaria							64	68	
Bosnia and Herzegovina							50	54	49
Croatia							70	74	70
FYROM							51	56	50
Yugoslavia[a]							50		
Serbia								52	46
Montenegro								57	52
Kosovo									40
Albania							40	45	41
Ukraine							57	62	62
Turkey							38	37	40

Percentage 'in favour'.
[a]In the year 2005 named 'Serbia and Montenegro'. NMS, new member states.
Source: Eurobarometer autumn surveys, weighted data

of Europeans in 2006. The readiness to accept new member countries from east and south-east Europe has generally increased in the course of the last five years. A very different situation is observed for Turkey. The approval for this country to join the EU remains around 30 per cent for the whole time period covered. Although the potential membership of Turkey has been an issue for many years already, it is less welcome than the other countries mentioned before.

Looking at the general picture, however, one can imagine a certain fatigue among the western EU members to extend their union each time to more and geographically distant countries. Although approval rates have increased slightly over time, only Croatia is approved by a majority of EU-15 citizens. The new member countries display by and large the same preference order of countries as the old member states, but show generally higher approval rates. Only a small number of potential member countries falls repeatedly below the majority threshold, namely Albania and Turkey as well as Kosovo (newly asked in 2008). The new members may take advantage from the smaller geographical distance and the broader experience with the relevant countries from Soviet times. It seems plausible that the new members need to play a bridging role when it comes to integrating more eastern members into the political community of the EU.

Summary

Over the past centuries, the common cultural and political roots of the people of Europe could seldom prevent long-standing hostilities from violent eruption. It was only after World War II that political elites started to initiate the process of European integration which deliberately aimed at creating a common framework of social and political identifications. The political-institutional success of these efforts is obvious. But how about its social basis? Have the people of Europe grown together into a political community; is there a 'sense of community' among EU citizens? The general answer is yes. Over half a century after World War II, a majority of EU citizens identifies with the new political community in the European Union.

Lacking pertinent and comparable survey information for most of this fifty-year period, we cannot determine when and how these identifications came into being. However, based on our findings from the analysis of available data, we must assume that they have been growing slowly. Over the last decade or so, there was not much of a secular change in European identifications; seasonal effects prevailed. If we drew a map of European Union identifications in the early 2000s, a centre–periphery picture would come to the fore. The highest level of identifications exists in the six original member countries, closely followed by European South; the further away one gets from this core of the Union in geographical and/or temporal terms, the weaker identifications become.

Majorities of EU citizens trust the people of other member countries. The people of the new member countries in Central and Eastern Europe, however, are still less trusted, and Turks are trusted the least. Figures on trust as well as on readiness to accept new members show that European citizens have a rather clear-cut mental map of the Union, a shared understanding of who is alike and who is different. The new Eastern member countries are still considered different; the East–West continental divide remains detectable. It will take a while for them to be fully integrated and accepted in the European ingroup. An additional but somewhat minor difference is commonly seen between people from the North and the South of Europe. A common view of all members is, however, that Turkey is clearly different from what is considered European.

Notes

1. This is an updated and revised version of a chapter that was originally published by the first author (Scheuer 1999).
2. This is not to say that states must be linguistically homogeneous; Belgium and Switzerland are obvious examples of nation-states that are not. However, in order to meet democratic requirements, every citizen must be able to communicate with state authorities in his or her own language (Bundesverfassungsgericht 1993, 438). This implies in places that there is more than one official language (such as three in Belgium and four in Switzerland).
3. Question wording: 'Do you ever think of yourself not only as a [nationality] citizen but also as a citizen of Europe? Often, sometimes, never'.
4. Question wording: 'In the near future do you see yourself as [nationality] only, [nationality] and European, European and [nationality], or European only?'.
5. Question wording: 'European Union Member States are "European citizens". Are you personally proud or not to be a "European citizen"? Would you say that you are very proud, fairly proud, not very proud, or not at all proud?'.
6. Question wording: 'I would like to ask you a question about how much trust you have in people from various countries. For each, please tell me whether you have a lot of trust, some trust, not very much trust, or no trust at all'.
7. Modified question wording: 'For each, please tell me whether you tend to trust them or tend not to trust them'.
8. Question wording: 'Now I would like to ask you a question about how much trust you have in people from various countries. Can you please tell me for each, whether you have a lot of trust of them or not very much trust. If you do not know a country well enough, just say so and I will go on to the next. How about the Austrians: do have a lot of trust of them or not very much trust?'.
9. In order to avoid distortion through composition effects, over-time changes are calculated on the basis of EU-15 countries only.
10. Question wording: 'For each of the following countries, would you be in favour or against it becoming part of the European Union in the future?'.

References

Bosch, Agusti, and Kenneth Newton. 1995. Economic calculus or familiarity breeds content?. In Niedermayer and Sinnott 1995, 73–104.

Bundesverfassungsgericht. 1993. Urteil vom 12. Oktober 1993. *Europäische Grundrechte Zeitschrift* 20, no. 17: 429–46.

Dalton, Russell J., and Richard C. Eichenberg. 1992. A people's Europe: Citizen support for the 1992 project and beyond. In *The 1992 project and the future of integration in Europe*, eds. Dale L. Smith and James Lee Ray, 73–91. Armonk: M.E. Sharpe.

De Vreese, Claes H. 2003. *Framing Europe. Television news and European integration*. Amsterdam: aksant.

Deutsch, Karl W., Sidney A. Burrell, and Robert A. Kann. 1957. *Political community and the North Atlantic area*. Princeton, NJ: Princeton Univ. Press.

Easton, David A. 1965. *A systems analysis of political life*. New York: John Wiley, repr. 1967, 1979.

Easton, David A. 1975. A re-assessment of the concept of political support. *British Journal of Political Science* 5: 435–57.

Eichenberg, Richard C., and Russell J. Dalton. 1993. Europeans and the European Community: The dynamics of public support for European integration. *International Organization* 47, no. 4: 507–34.

Koopmans, Ruud, and Jessica Erbe. 2004. Towards a European sphere? Vertical and horizontal dimensions of Europeanized political communication. *Innovation* 17, no. 2: 97–118.

Kuhnle, Stein. 1993. Citizenship. In *The Blackwell encyclopaedia of political science*, ed. Vernon Bogdanor, 94–5. Oxford: Basil Blackwell.

Lilli, Waldemar. 1998. Europäische Identität: Chance und Risiken ihrer Verwirklichung aus einer sozialpsychologischen Grundlagenperspektive. In *Europa der Bürger? Voraussetzungen, Alternativen, Konsequenzen*, eds. Thomas König, Elmar Rieger and Hermann Schmitt, 139–58. Mannheimer Jahrbuch für Europäische Sozialforschung 3. Frankfurt am Main: Campus.

Lindberg, Leon N., and Stuart A. Scheingold, eds. 1970. *Europe's would-be polity: Patterns of change in the European Community*. Englewood Cliffs, NJ: Prentice Hall.

Mintzel, Alf. 1997. *Multikulturelle Gesellschaften in Europa und Nordamerika: Konzepte, Streitfragen, Analysen, Befunde*. Passau: Wissenschaftsverlag Rothe.

Niedermayer, Oskar. 1995. Trust and sense of community. In Niedermayer and Sinnott 1995, 227–45.

Niedermayer, Oskar. 1997. Die Entwicklung der öffentlichen Meinung zu Europa, Beitrag zum Forschungsprojekt 'Der Wandel europapolitischer Grundverständnisse', Berlin.

Niedermayer, Oskar, and Richard Sinnott, eds. 1995. *Public opinion and internationalized governance*. Oxford: Oxford Univ. Press.

Pfetsch, Frank R. 1997. *Die Europäische Union: Geschichte, Institutionen, Prozesse: Eine Einführung*. München: Fink.

Risse, Thomas. 2003. The Euro between national and European identity. *Journal of European Public Policy* 10, no. 4: 487–505.

Scharpf, Fritz. 1999. *Governing in Europe: Efficient and democratic?*. Oxford: Oxford Univ. Press.

Scheuer, Angelika. 1999. A political community?. In *Political participation and legitimacy in the European Union*, eds. Hermann Schmitt and Jacques Thomassen, 25–46. Oxford: Oxford Univ. Press.

Scheuer, Angelika. 2005. *How Europeans see Europe. Structure and dynamics of European legitimacy beliefs*. Amsterdam: Vossiuspers.

Schmitt, Hermann. 2005. Political linkage in the European Union. In *Political parties and political systems. The concept of linkage revisited*, eds. David Farrell, Piero Ignazi and Andrea Römmele, 145–58. New York: Praeger.

Schmitt, Hermann, and Helga Treiber-Reif. 1990. Structure in European attitudes, Report on behalf of the Cellule de Prospective of the Commission of the European Communities. Mannheim: ZEUS.

Stråth, Bo. 2002. A European identity: To the historical limits of a concept. *European Journal of Social Theory* 5, no. 4: 387–501.

Tajfel, Henry, and John C. Turner. 1986. The social identity theory of inter-group behavior. In *Psychology of intergroup relations*, eds. Stephan Worchel and William G. Austin, 7–24. Chicago: Nelson-Hall.

Appendix A

Table A1.   Those who consider themselves as European citizens, 1992–2007

	1992	1993	1994	1995	1996	1997	1998	1999	2000	2001	2002	2003	2004	2005	2007
Belgium	58	65	66	61	50	47	53	56	56	52	62	54	62	64	69
France	67	65	75	68	63	64	64	59	62	63	65	63	68	66	67
Germany	55	54	66	60	47	48	49	49	54	57	60	61	61	63	69
Italy	69	70	71	73	62	63	68	71	73	66	77	72	65	61	44
Luxembourg	69	63	76	75	71	73	67	72	73	75	74	74	66	74	76
The Netherlands	56	59	65	60	57	57	57	56	57	54	58	54	59	65	70
Denmark	51	50	51	46	42	44	49	44	47	59	62	62	58	60	62
UK	43	37	48	42	37	38	35	30	31	28	34	33	38	34	38
Ireland	46	49	58	53	47	47	45	44	47	43	53	47	53	47	40
Greece	60	56	54	47	38	46	46	40	44	41	49	48	43	53	51
Spain	60	55	61	55	54	52	60	63	70	59	67	65	61	58	62
Portugal	58	52	55	53	46	39	37	47	48	47	53	49	51	55	48
Austria				46	44		47	51	48	52	55	48	51	52	54
Finland				47	40		45	38	41	40	44	42	42	51	51
Sweden			59	38	34		39	37	40	48	47	47	46	56	54
Cyprus (south)													69	69	61
Malta													66	71	66
Poland													54	59	54
Czech Republic													42	61	50
Slovakia													61	60	55
Hungary													35	49	54
Slovenia													55	64	63
Estonia													54	48	51
Latvia													51	54	43

Table A1.   (*Continued*)

	1992	1993	1994	1995	1996	1997	1998	1999	2000	2001	2002	2003	2004	2005	2007
Lithuania													43	44	42
Bulgaria													54	42	50
Romania													53	56	42
Turkey													28	22	
Cyprus (north)													48		
Croatia													63	66	
Original 6[a]	62	62	69	65	56	57	59	58	62	61	66	64	64	63	62
1st extension[b]		39	49	43	38	39	37	32	33	31	37	36	41	37	40
2nd extension[c]	60	55	59	53	50	49	53	56	61	54	62	59	56	57	58
3rd extension[d]				43	39		43	42	44	47	49	47	47	54	53
4th extension[e]													50	57	53
5th extension[f]														55	44

'Only European', 'European and national' and 'national and European'.
[a]Belgium, The Netherlands, Luxembourg, France, Germany, Italy.
[b]UK, Ireland, Denmark.
[c]Greece, Spain, Portugal.
[d]Austria, Finland, Sweden.
[e]Cyprus, Malta, Poland, Czech Republic, Slovakia, Hungary, Slovenia, Estonia, Latvia, Lithuania.
[f]Bulgaria, Romania.
Source: Eurobarometer, weighted data (national weight for country figures, EU-weight for country groups).

Table A2.   Mokken scaling of European pride and identifications as a European citizen

	H-value
The Netherlands	0.77
Finland	0.76
Northern Ireland	0.74
Cyprus	0.69
Estonia	0.69
Italy	0.66
Latvia	0.66
Czech Republic	0.65
Austria	0.64
Slovakia	0.64
Ireland	0.60
Belgium	0.58
Britain	0.53
Denmark	0.53
Hungary	0.52
Slovenia	0.52
Poland	0.49
France	0.46
Luxembourg	0.46
Portugal	0.46
Germany	0.43
Spain	0.42
Greece	0.41

Source: European Election Study (EES) 2004. Mokken scaling tests for the unidimensionality of a set of items. Meaning of H-values: below 0.30 = no scale, above 0.30 = a weak scale, above 0.40 = a medium scale, and above 0.50 = a strong scale.

The EU Party System after Eastern Enlargement

HERMANN SCHMITT* & JACQUES THOMASSEN**

*MZES, University of Mannheim, Mannheim, Germany; **School of Management and Government, University of Twente, Enschede, The Netherlands

ABSTRACT   This paper investigates whether and how the process of Eastern enlargement of the European Union has altered the EU party system. This process has added representatives of some forty new parties to the previous structure. Comparing party placements on the two main dimensions of political contestation in the EU — the left–right dimension and integration–independence dimension — it is found that Eastern enlargement did surprisingly little to the format of the party system and the stature of its political groups, both regarding their distinctiveness and their cohesion.

Introduction

The object of our research, the EU party system, needs some initial conceptual elaboration before we can address the central research questions of this contribution. It manifests itself most visibly in the European Parliament. There, nationally elected MEPs form political groups based on ideological vicinity and issue congruence rather than — as one could expect — nationality. This parliament has been able to increase its powers considerably over the past two decades. Today it is a powerful co-legislator on a par with the European Council in the passage of roughly two-thirds of all EU legislative acts (directives). Those EU directives are ultimately transformed into national law in every single of the now twenty-seven EU member countries.

But what, in fact, is the EU party system? It is widely accepted that a party system consists of the relevant parties that are operating in a political system

Correspondence Address: Hermann Schmitt, MZES, University of Mannheim, D-68131 Mannheim, Germany. E-mail: hschmitt@mzes.uni-mannheim.de plus the relations they have with one another (Sartori 1976). This definition gains complexity, however, when applied to the multi-level system of governance of the European Union.[1] What is a European Union party? Whether or not something like an EU party exists at all depends on the definition of 'party'. Following again Giovanni Sartori, we think of a party as a socio-political entity that 'presents at elections, and is capable of placing through elections, candidates for public office' (Sartori 1976, 63). According to that, EU parties might be said not to exist because the EP electoral process — candidate selection, campaigning and vote choice — is mainly organized nationally. But what if national and local member parties of EU parties in their place nominate candidates and in national and local campaigns compete for votes, does this harm the notion of EU parties, of a EU party system and of EU-wide party competition?[2] We argue that organizational decentralization as such does not obstruct the integrity and effectiveness of EU-wide parties as long as their ideological and behavioural cohesion is not compromised (Lord 2006). Local autonomy and regional variation is a fact of life in many national party systems — perhaps most obviously so in federal systems — and must not be seen as standing in the way of the proper functioning of an encompassing EU party system.

If we then accept the notion of a multi-level party system, with some functions allocated in local party organizations, others at the national level, and still others at the level of the European Union, the question of compatibility of the different layers of the party system arises. Erecting an overall EU party system upon those of the EU member countries obviously requires some basic structural similarity between them. One school of thought argues, in the Rokkanian tradition, that this compatibility has been granted in the past by a roughly similar cleavage structure, which gave western European party systems their particular shape (Lipset and Rokkan 1967). At the time of suffrage expansion, i.e. at a time when social cleavages were first translated into electoral alliances, the basic and most salient socio-political conflict was fought between industrial labour and capital. This has led almost everywhere to the formation of labour unions and, in the political and parliamentary sphere, of a labour party (or a socialist or social democratic party) which opposed the liberal and conservative (or Christian-democratic) forces that were more or less closely allied with entrepreneurial interests. Other, older, socio-political conflicts — the one between the primary and secondary sector; between church and state; or between centre and periphery — have also contributed to the characteristic form of west European party systems. While there is considerable variation in the national cleavage structures upon which west European party systems have been build, the commonalities between them have been strong enough to support a EU-wide 'super structure' that successfully aggregates, in a few EU-wide parties, almost every national party gaining representation in the elections to the European Parliament — irrespective of obvious differences between governmental status and participation in coalition governments in which these parties are involved nationally.

On 1 May 2004, eight post-communist party systems (plus those of Cyprus and Malta) were added to the EU party system by what was called the 'eastward enlargement' of the European Union. Roughly six weeks later, in mid-June, the members of the European Parliament were directly elected. This time, about 350 million EU citizens from twenty-five member countries were entitled to vote. The question that we will pursue in the rest of this contribution is whether these new post-communist party systems are sufficiently similar to the western European 'model' so that they can easily fit into the new environment. Put another way, we are asking whether the eastward enlargement might have weakened the EU party system — characteristic dimensions of its strength having been the relative concentration of the party system, and the distinctiveness and cohesion of its constituent parts.

In pursuing this research question we will (a) recapitulate the major developments of the EU party system prior to Eastern enlargement, (b) review what is known about the evolution of Eastern European party systems after the collapse of communism, and (c) discuss the dimensionality of EU party competition. We then move on and (d) present the strategy of our analyses and the database we utilize and (e) our findings.

The EU Party System Before 1 May 2004

During its first five decades, the EU party system was a remarkably efficient device for integrating a host of new entrants into a rather 'lean' structure.[3] The basic design of it was established already in 1953 when, in the Common Assembly of the European Coal and Steel Community, Christian-democrats, socialists and liberals established the first transnational parliamentary groups. From the very beginning of the European project, just eight years after the end of the Second World War, national political parties were organizing their European co-operation on the basis of common socio-political roots and ideological proximity rather than nationality.

New entrants to be integrated in the early defined European party system came from nine additional member countries, which joined the original six between 1973 and 1996.[4] But also 'really new' parties that emerged in the existing member countries eventually entered parliament.[5]

The year 1973 was a turbulent one for what is now called the EU party system: three new political groups were built. A communist group was formed out of French (PCF) and Italian (PCI) deputies. In 1989, with the breakdown of communism and some time ahead of the collapse of the post-WWII party system of Italy in 1992, this group lost the main successor-party of the PCI (the Italian PDS) to the Socialist Group, leaving the French communists with some new 'far left'-acquisitions (the German PDS, among others) in a severely diminished far-left group.

Still in 1973, British Conservatives (and allies) and French Gaullists (and allies) formed a new political group each. Due to their different social roots and political perspectives (not least on matters of European integration), both did not easily fit into the Christian-democratic EPP. Yet the draw of this powerful agglomeration of EP members eventually overcame these socio-political obstacles: The British and Danish conservatives associated themselves with the EPP in 1992 (following the Spanish conservatives who already had joined the EPP in 1989), and the Gaullist RPR joined after the 1994 European Parliament election.

All of these parties institutionalize socio-political conflicts that originate in the more or less distant past. But European Parliament elections also helped the new party family[6] of the Greens to establish itself. The first Green deputies entered parliament after the European Parliament election of 1984 and settled with a rather heterogeneous 'Rainbow Group'. One election later, in 1989, the Greens became numerous enough to build a readily identifiable ecologist group which has gained representation in every parliament since.

Christian-democrats and conservatives, socialists, liberals, the far left and the greens — together they define the basic structure of the EU party system. There are two additional groups right-of-centre that aggregate Euro-critical views of different rigour, the Europe of Democracies and Diversities (EDD, which became the Independence and Democracy Group after the 2004 election), and the Union for a Europe of Nations (EoN). Both groups are of about equal size; they compete with one another for members of the same ideological background, and one might assume that in the long run only one of the two will prevail. And there is finally the group of the 'Non Inscrits' which traditionally has been dominated by extreme-right members.[7]

Just before Eastern enlargement, the EU party system integrated about 130 national parties in not more than five consolidated party groups, and in two less consolidated but minor 'ideological areas' — the euro-sceptic right-of-centre, and the far-right. And these numbers, small as they are, still give a false impression of the format of the EU party system which is essentially characterized by two predominant political groups — the PES on the left, and the EPP on the right.

In the world of party systems at least, small numbers are good numbers. They signify governability, centripetal competition, alternation of governments, accountability — all the good things of the two-party model of governance are associated with them. The format of the EU party system which goes all the way back to the Common Assembly of the ECSC of 1953 should therefore not stand in the way of a democratic EU polity.

But, of course, the democratic potential of a party system does not only depend on a small numbers of parties and on party system concentration. It also depends on the distinctiveness and cohesion of its partisan actors. Here, as well, empirical analyses of political preferences and behaviours of samples of EP voters and of various branches of party elites (Schmitt and Thomassen 1999); content analyses of political parties' election programmes issued at the occasion of European Parliament elections (Thomassen and Schmitt 2004; Wüst and Schmitt 2007); and roll-call analyses of the votes of members of this parliament (Hix 2002; Kreppel and Hix 2003; Hix, Noury, and Roland 2006) all have revealed that this party system works surprisingly 'normally'. No matter what data source is analysed, political groups are 'distinct', which is to say that they differ from one another in policy and ideological terms. And, despite their enormous performance in integrating new members, these groups are also astonishingly 'cohesive', which is to say that their constituent parts are comparatively similar in policy and ideological terms. What is more, distinct and cohesive EP groups base their parliamentary vote increasingly upon ideological closeness. It seems that 'grand coalition' strategies that were pursued in the past by the two major players of the system, the EPP and the PES in order to increase the powers of the parliament *vis-à-vis* the council, have become less popular (Kreppel and Hix 2003; Hix, Noury, and Roland 2006). In short, this party system was 'ready for power' (Hix 2002) at the time of the sixth European Paliament election of June 2004. This election added about forty Central and Eastern European parties to the EU system, thus elevating the overall number to some 170 national parties sending delegations to the European Parliament.

The Party Systems of East Central Europe — Do They Fit In?

The basic structure of West European party systems has been defined by socio-political cleavages. These cleavages were translated into partisan alignments more or less at the time when universal suffrage was achieved. In most places, this happened around the late nineteenth and the early twentieth centuries. But what about the central and east European systems that democratized — or re-democratized (Ágh 1998) — only in the early 1990s? As a matter of fact, competitive party systems emerged very rapidly in these countries. But do they rest upon socio-political cleavages, or on less stable pillars, such as specific issue alliances or the personal charisma of political elites that predominated during regime change?

The latter assumption, sometimes referred to as the *tabula rasa* theory, has received little empirical support (Kitschelt et al. 1999). Actually, there seems to be a stable structure of social divisions (Evans and Whitefield 2000), while the political sphere is still characterized by substantial levels of volatility both on the voters' and the parties' side (e.g. Birch 2001). This reminds us of the fact that social divisions are necessary but not sufficient conditions for socio-political cleavages. As Bartolini and Mair (1990, 216) have put it: 'Social divisions become cleavages when they are organised as such'. Organization requires time, resources and opportunities, all of which might not yet have been sufficiently available in post-communist democracies. In addition, the formation of cleavages also requires political elites who actively promote the partisan organisation of social divisions. Under present-day conditions of mass political communication, however, this is not necessarily always in their own best interest.[8]

For quite different reasons, then, socio-political cleavages in Central and Eastern Europe are probably less developed than is sometimes claimed (e.g. Bakke and Sitter 2005; a bit more implicitly also Whitefield 2002). But this is not to say that social conflicts do not contribute to ideological divisions which, finally, may be represented politically by various, and varying, partisan actors.

Dimensions of Party Competition in the European Union

Before we go on and test the actual fit between parties and party systems from old and new EU member countries in the European Parliament after the

2004 election, we need to be clear about what we want to look at. There is a considerable literature on the dimensionality of the European party space.[9] Gabel and Hix (2002) and Gabel and Anderson (2002) identify some variant of the left–right scheme as the one dimension that structures the European political space. For Hix and Lord (1997) and Schmitt and Thomassen (2000), two orthogonal dimensions structure the European political space: these are the left–right axis and a dimension of EU support or opposition.[10] Others, like Gary Marks *cum suis*, arrive at a three-dimensional picture of ideological divisions: economic left–right, new politics, and again the dimension of EU support (e.g. Marks et al. 2006).

Some of this scholarly dissent may originate in technicalities — in different methods applied, different sorts of data used, and so on.[11] This certainly calls for a critical evaluation. However, rather than methodologically, we will proceed conceptually. We propose that the issues that are dealt with at the EU level of the European multi-level system fall into two categories: constitutional issues and ordinary ones (Schmitt and Thomassen 1999). Constitutional issues are about the structure of the evolving political system of the European Union. The relations between parliament, commission and council are part of it; enlargements and the question of admission of new members are another; the constitutional process and EU treaties more generally are a third; more examples could be added easily. These constitutional issues are not about EU policies, but about the EU polity. A characteristic point of dissent is about more or less integration.

In contrast to these constitutional struggles, ordinary issues are about concrete policies. They tend to (but do not have to) assume a multi-level nature in the sense that they are discussed and dealt with at various levels of the EU multi-level political system. Examples are the economy, the welfare state, the environment, and so on. For those 'ordinary' issues, an 'ordinary' measure of ideological conflict should apply. The most prominent of those is the left–right dimension. A wide variety of conflicts relate to it: political (equality vs. hierarchy), economic (poor vs. rich), religious (abstainers vs. believers), and time-orientated (change vs. continuity) (see Laponce 1981; also Bobbio 1996). Due to the 'imperialistic' character of this ideological scheme (Fuchs and Klingemann 1990), the connotations of left and right (or, put another way, the alliances of political oppositions with either the left or the right ideological camp) are changing through history. But the impetus of the ideological archetypes seems to prevail: a leftist perspective favours political change towards more equality, while a rightist perspective defends individual liberties and tries to keep things as they are or move them back.

The change in the meaning elements of the left–right political code is particularly pronounced in times of rapid social change when traditional socio-political conflicts are weakening and new controversies are assuming their place.[12] In those phases, the contours of what 'left' and 'right' means become fuzzy, and doubts arise about the utility of these spatial archetypes. Quite typically, during those turbulent times, notions like 'the new politics' (late 1970s), 'the new left' (1980s) or 'the new right' (1990s) become fashionable. A few years later, 'new politics' are not so new anymore and what once was 'the new left' or 'the new right' has become a regular component of the left–right political code. Therefore, we do not follow the work of Hooghe and Marks (Hooghe, Marks, and Wilson 2002; Marks et al. 2006). In the present contribution, we refrain from distinguishing different dimensions of the left–right divide and concentrate on the one overarching ideological cleavage.[13] Together with the EU dimension (furthering vs. moving back European integration), these are the two ideological dimensions that structure party competition in the European Parliament (see for empirical support McElroy and Benoit 2007) and that we will focus on in the following analysis.

Data

Before we can finally move on and test the fit between parties and party systems from old and new EU member countries in the European Parliament, we need to say a word on the data we analyse. We start out with a look at official election statistics. The core of our empirical evidence, however, comes from other sources. We utilize three of them: the post-electoral surveys of the European Election Study 2004; a content-analysis of the manifestos of political parties issued ahead of the European Parliament election (the so-called 'Euromanifestos'), and the 2002 expert survey on national parties and the European Union (the 2002 Chappell Hill expert survey).

With regard to the voter survey, we analyse popular perceptions of the location of nationally relevant parties on the left–right dimension[14] and the pro–anti-EU dimension.[15] We do so by computing measures of central tendency (arithmetic means) of voter perceptions of party positions and interpret these measures as indicators of true party locations.[16] Essentially, then, our units of analysis are political parties and the positions they assume on the left–right and the pro–anti-EU dimension. This reduces the number of cases that we are dealing with from some 25,000 (respondents) to 131 (parties represented in the EP and covered by the 2004 European Election Study).

The second source of information utilized is a content analysis of the 2004 EP election programmes of the parties (Euromanifestos). As for national election programmes of political parties, these Euromanifestos must be understood as authoritative statements of the issue emphasis and the policy goals of the party that publishes them. The analysis of those documents generally follows the MRG (in later parlance, CMP) tradition. The Euromanifesto coding scheme (EMCS) is very close but not identical to this familiar MRG/CMP coding scheme. Major additions to it consist of a new domain — the EU polity with a number of subcategories — and an additional code characterizing the 'governmental frame'[17] of each meaning element that is coded. The EMCS was applied to the EP election programmes of political parties by national expert-coders. We use two additive indices for estimating party positions on the left–right and the pro–anti-integration dimension: the familiar RILE-index popularized by the CMP dataset (Budge et al. 2001), and a parallel instrument adding positive and subtracting negative statements in the new EU domain that was added to the CMP coding scheme.

The final dataset we use is based on an expert survey. The Chappell Hill 2002 expert survey dataset provides data on party positions on European integration for 171 parties in twenty-three of the twenty-five current EU member states (not Luxembourg and Estonia) as well as in Bulgaria and Romania. The survey was administered between September 2002 and April 2003 to 636 academics specializing in parties, European integration or closely related topics in one of the countries considered. The number of surveys completed was 238, which amounts to a 37 per cent response rate. We again use the general left–right placement of parties[18] and their positioning on European integration.[19]

In order to determine the effect of Eastern enlargement on the EU party system, we will compare the distinctiveness and cohesion of EP groups before and after enlargement. One way of doing this is to determine the effect of EP group membership of national parties and their 'post-communist newness' on their issue positions: if the new members are systematically holding different views, this post-communist newness should play a major role. Another strategy of analysis is a direct comparison of the issue positions of old and new member parties within the different EP groups by way of scatterplots: if the new members are different, the groups should find themselves more or less 'off' the diagonal. A third and final way is an analysis of the ideological structure of the newly elected parliament: do we still find the horseshoe-like distribution of groups in the two-dimensional ideological space that characterized the EU party competition so far? All three steps are taken on the basis of all our three data sources: voter surveys, manifesto content codes, and the expert survey.[20] Before we proceed on this, however, we will first take a closer look at the election results that constituted the 2004 European Parliament.

Findings

The 2004 Election Result — East and West Compared

We begin with a look at official election result figures. The question we are trying to answer is: how different was the eastern vote? We distinguish between votes that were given to any of the parties affiliated with an EP group ('any EP group'), votes that were given to a party that gained representation but did not join one of the groups ('non-inscrits'), votes that were given to a party that did not master the threshold of representation ('not represented') and, finally, those that abstained ('non voters'). The result of our computations is obvious: 'Post-communist' citizens are heavily over-represented among non-voters and among voters of parties that did *not* join an EP group, while they are clearly under-represented in the electorates of parties that did join one of the established political groups of the European Parliament. The proportion of unrepresented votes is virtually identical in East and West (Table 1).

But this is not the only perspective to apply. Comparing the vote shares that the different groups of the European Parliament received in the 'old' and

Table 1. EP voting behaviour, West and East (millions of EU citizens)

	Any organized EP group	'Non Inscrits'	Not represented	Non voters	Entitled to vote
EU-15 + Cyprus and Malta	125.2 (92.0)	9.6 (78.7)	8.5 (83.3)	148.3 (77.9)	291.6 (83.6)
Eight post-communist countries	10.8 (8.0)	2.6 (21.3)	1.7 (16.7)	42.0 (22.1)	57.1 (16.4)
EU-25	136.0 (100)	12.2 (100)	10.2 (100)	190.3 (100)	348.7 (100)

Column percentages in parentheses.
Source: Official statistics as published on the web pages of the European Parliament as well as by www.europa-digital.de, www.parties-and-elections.de, and www.electionworld.org.

the 'new Europe', we find that EPP–ED support is somewhat stronger in the East, while PES and far left support is considerably weaker there. Support for liberal parties is almost identical. The same holds for EU-sceptical parties (taking EoN and I&D members together): vote shares are limited in the West and in the East, and certainly much less dramatic than some authors suggested (e.g. Beichelt 2004). Quite spectacular, however, is the lack of a green electorate among post-communist voters and, as we have seen before, the fact that many of the Eastern voters elected representatives who could not decide which parliamentary party to join (Table 2).

Elevated shares of non-voters and a high proportion of votes for 'unaffiliated' representatives are, perhaps, the clearest signs of a less than perfect fit between still-consolidating Eastern European party systems and the super-structure of the EU party system (Schmitt 2005). Eastern European party systems are still somewhat less inclusive than their Western counterparts — turnout in first-order national elections prior to the European Parliament election was at 63 per cent on average, some 15 per cent lower than in the West. But not only is participation lower, those who participate are different.

Table 2. Distribution of votes between EP groups (millions of voters of parties that gained EP representation)

	EPP-ED	PES	Lib	Green	Far Left	I&D	EoN	Non-inscrits	All
EU-15 + Cyprus and Malta	49.3 (36.3)	37.3 (27.5)	11.8 (8.7)	10.1 (7.4)	9.2 (6.8)	3.4 (2.5)	5.0 (3.7)	9.6 (7.1)	135.7 (100)
Eight post-communist member countries	5.4 (40.4)	2.7 (20.1)	1.1 (8.2)	0.1 (0.7)	0.5 (3.7)	0.0 (0.0)	1.0 (7.4)	2.6 (19.5)	13.4 (100)
EU-25	54.7 (36.8)	40.0 (26.8)	12.9 (8.7)	10.2 (6.8)	9.7 (6.5)	3.4 (2.2)	6.0 (4.0)	12.2 (8.2)	149.1 (100)

Row percentages in parentheses
Source: Official statistics as published on the web pages of the European Parliament as well as by www.europa-digital.de, www.parties-and-elections.de, and www.electionworld.org.

Volatility figures reveal that party alignments of post-communist voters are still much more fluid: an average of 37 per cent of 'aggregate vote switches' suggest that, in the two previous first-order elections, almost every second Eastern voter supported different parties; this compares to only 11 per cent in the West of the EU. Weaker party alignments and higher volatility finally translate into a higher fragmentation of post-communist party systems — this is at least what the comparison of the effective number of parties ahead of the 2004 EP election suggests: the eight Eastern party systems comprise, on average, 5.5 effective parties, as compared to 4.2 effective parties in the West of the European Union (Table 3).

The European Union Party System Before and After Enlargement

As we have already seen, the 2004 election of the European Parliament has strengthened the Christian-conservative group, and it has weakened the left, broadly speaking. Eastern enlargement has significantly contributed to these developments. But, over and above the political result of the election, did enlargement change the structure of the party system? Are EP groups less distinct and cohesive afterwards? And what about the structure of party competition?

Our first approach to answering these questions is an effort to predict issue positions of political parties on the basis of their group membership and their post-communist newness. Table 4 shows the results of this enterprise. At least three observations are worth mentioning. First, and most importantly in our context, we know quite a lot about the issue positions of political parties if we know which EP group they have joined; their post-communist background (or otherwise), however, hardly affects their issue orientations. Secondly, left–right positions are better explained by our two predictors than

Table 3.   Inclusiveness, stability and concentration of the twenty-five national party systems

	Turnout previous national election	Volatility previous pair of national elections	Effective number of parties previous national election
EU-15 + Cyprus and	78.1	11.0	4.2
Malta	11.8	6.8	1.6
Eight post-communist	62.6	37.1	5.5
member countries	9.5	19.4	1.8
EU-25	73.1	19.4	4.6
	13.2	17.2	1.7
sig. (F)	0.004	0.000	0.068

Means and standard deviations.
Source: Official statistics as published by www.europa-digital.de, www.parties-and-elections.de and www.electionworld.org. Note that our concept of volatility considers voters to switch if they vote in two consecutive elections for parties with different names, no matter whether these parties are mergers/splinters of previously separate/united parties; compare Sikk (2001) for a different view.

Table 4. Ideological positions of political parties represented in the 2004 European Parliament as predicted by group affiliation and 'post-communist newness'

	Left–Right			Pro–Anti-Europe		
	eta	beta	RSQ	eta	beta	RSQ
Voter perceptions (*n*=668)						
– EP group affiliation	0.89	0.90		0.73	0.74	
– post-communist newness	0.11	0.04		0.09	0.17	
			0.79			0.55
Manifesto content (*n*=692)						
– EP group affiliation	0.66	0.66		0.59	0.60	
– post-communist newness	0.09	0.00		0.03	0.07	
			0.43			0.36
Expert judgements (*n*=639)						
– EP group affiliation	0.89	0.91		0.70	0.72	
– post-communist newness	0.16	0.06		0.07	0.07	
			0.80			0.50

Analyses of variance — MCA results.
Party positions are weighted with (multiplied by) the number of EP representatives of respective parties.

pro–anti-Europe positions. Thirdly, all three data sources tell the same story, with almost identical results for voter and expert surveys and similar but somewhat weaker coefficients from the analysis of Euromanifestoes data. Note that these findings are largely independent of the weighting decision: whether we count each party observation only once, or as many times as its delegation size suggests, hardly affects the results.

This first and somewhat global test suggests that an Eastern background does not affect the position that political parties take on the left–right and the pro–anti-integration dimension. As these are the two major issue dimensions structuring the EU political space, this can only mean that Eastern enlargement has done surprisingly little to the EU party system. With or without the new members — the EP groups look very much the same, both with regard to their left–right and their pro–anti-Europe position. Central and Eastern European origin and thus a post-communist background of parties hardly imply a different worldview, and the new parties seem to fit very well in the existing structure.

We move on to a second test and confront for each party group the average issue positions of old and new members. Figure 1 summarizes the results. It presents six scatterplots that confront the mean left–right and pro–anti-Europe position of new and old members, for each of our three data sources. The degree of distinctiveness is indicated by the range of positions found in the (*z*-transformed) data; cohesiveness of new and old members is indicated by the concentration of party (EP group) positions around the regression slope and the resulting R^2. The general impression one gets from these six scatterplots is one of a remarkably distinctive and cohesive EU party system.

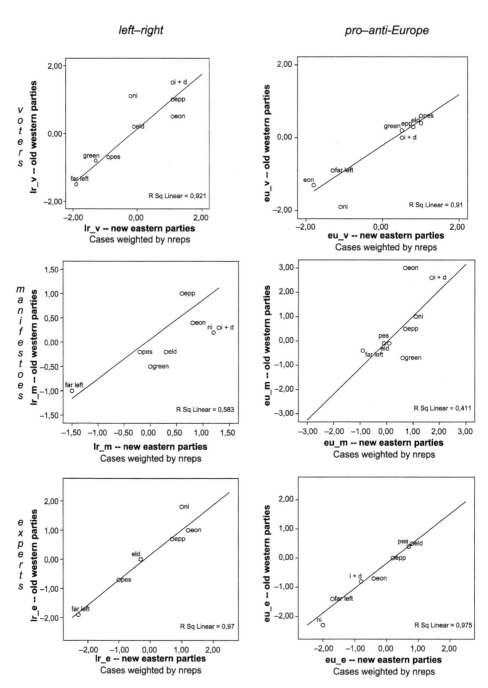

Figure 1. Ideological congruence of old and new members of EP groups (scatterplots, regression slopes and explained variance).

The spread of party positions is enormous, on both dimensions. PES and EPP, the two hegemonic parties of the system, offer clearly different left–right policies, while they are comparatively close with regard to the pro–anti-Europe dimension. This is so no matter what data source we consult.

Our results regarding the cohesiveness of parties vary somewhat between the three methods. Voter and expert surveys identify a rather close issue congruence between new and old members, while manifesto contents suggest a somewhat weaker fit. The same observation holds for the positioning of EP groups relative to one another: voter and expert surveys by and large reveal the same configuration, while the content data suggest a somewhat different structure.[21]

While Eastern enlargement did not affect the positioning of the EP groups along the left–right and the pro–anti-EU dimension, it still could have had an impact on the relation between these two basic dimensions of party competition in the European Parliament. In the past, there was all but consensus among scholars in this domain. The basic point of dissent has been whether left–right orientations determine pro–anti-Europe positions (e.g. Hooghe, Marks, and Wilson 2002), or whether the two are independent from and orthogonal towards one another (e.g. Hix and Lord 1997). All our different data sources suggest that the two dimensions are correlated only weakly, and that this correlation is virtually identical for Western and Eastern parties.

Based on the European Election Study data, Figure 2 displays this modest but significant association between the two variables graphically. It suggests

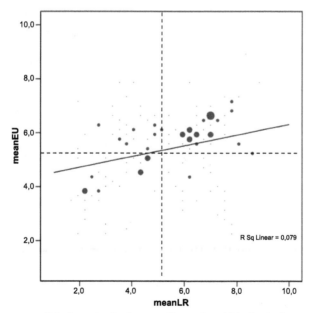

Figure 2.   European political parties in the two-dimensional ideological space after the 2004 European Parliament election.
Source: European Election Study 2004. *n* of cases (parties) = 158 from twenty-two member countries. The larger the dots in the graph, the more parties are located at this point.

that political parties have a somewhat higher chance of Euro-positive orientations the further to the right they are located. But the model fit is indeed very poor and one is probably right in describing the EU political space as two-dimensional, with left–right orientations and pro–anti-EU attitudes independently structuring it.

In the present context, in any case, the most important finding is that the two dimensions are as dependent or independent in Eastern as in Western parties. This also implies that the structure of party competition in the European Parliament was hardly affected by the 'big bang' of May 2004.

Figure 3 displays the familiar 'horseshoe': the gravity line of EU party competition first identified by Hix and Lord (1997). While there is a considerable spread of EP group positions along the left–right dimension, variation along the pro–anti-EU dimension is less pronounced. Nevertheless, far-left and far-right parties tend to be somewhat more sceptical about the European Union than centre-left and centre-right parties. The latter also tend to be the larger ones, which might have nurtured the impression that there was hardly any choice offered to the voter in European Parliament elections.

If we distinguished Eastern and Western member parties of EP groups and displayed them separately, the pictures would be much the same — with one significant difference though. The overall 'centre-right' location of the 'Non Inscrits (NI)' would be on the 'far right' for Western members only, and it would be in the 'centre' for new Eastern members only. If this 'technical group' is united by anything, it is certainly not by the left–right ideology.

Conclusion

Surprisingly enough, the EU party system has not changed much as a result of Eastern enlargement. The EPP–ED has gained additional strength, both PES and the Far Left suffered, and the proportion of unaffiliated members has increased due to the fact that a good number of Eastern members did not join one of the traditional political groups. However, the cohesiveness of EP groups did not visibly suffer from the addition of new 'post-communist' members, nor did the distinctiveness of the parties decline. The 'horseshoe'-like gravity line of EU party competition is very much the same before and after Eastern enlargement, with centre-left and centre-right groups more in favour of further integration than far-left and far-right groups.

Some party system consequences of eastward enlargement of the EU may not yet be fully visible. Eastern party systems are still in flux, with a limited reach of electoral politics in general, high levels of volatility among those who do participate, and a significantly greater diversity of partisan actors than in the West. To the degree that these transitory characteristics of Eastern party systems are declining, one might expect the Eastern vote to undergo significant changes in the future.

One expectation in particular was not born out by the election. In the political process of the new Eastern member countries, the issue of EU membership was much less politicized, and the strength of EU sceptical parties much less pronounced, than was predicted by many. Bielasiak (2004, 1) can probably

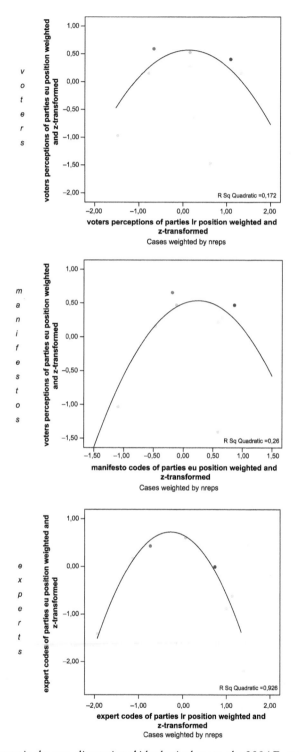

Figure 3. EP groups in the two-dimensional ideological space: the 2004 European Parliament.

explain part of it when he writes that '... there is a tension between the notion that the party systems of post-communism render the integration issue relevant to the competitive process, and the acknowledgement of a long-standing broad policy consensus on the "return to Europe"'. As a result, '... the integration question has remained largely a second-order political concern rather than a primary contestation issue in the charged competitive dimension of the former communist states' (*ibid.*, 22).

Putting the phenomena of below-average electoral participation and unsuccessful integration of elected members in established EP groups aside, the integration of the parties from the new countries seems to work out comparatively smoothly. Is this the case despite major ideological discrepancies, as Kreppel and Gungor (2004) propose? They argue that integration of the new members should cause little problem because they are all coming from backgrounds characterized by strong parliaments and weak parties — much as the EU parliamentary and party system. While this might be the case, our analysis has shown that ideology was not a major obstacle, but rather a catalyst for adaptation and integration.

Notes

1. See on multi-level systems of governance, König, Rieger, and Schmitt (1996) or Hooghe and Marks (2001), for example.
2. This suggests that Estonian or Portuguese EP candidates — to name just two geographically distant member nationalities — must not be selected in Brussels by a central party authority. In fact, there are good normative democratic reasons (going back to the participation rights of local party members and supporters) why they should not be selected centrally but locally (e.g. Abendroth 1964).
3. See, for the following, Henig (1979), Hix and Lord (1997) and the web pages of the political groups of the EP.
4. The parties of Ireland, Britain and Denmark entered the European Parliament in 1973; those of Greece in 1981; Spanish and Portuguese parties entered in 1983; Austrian, Finnish and Swedish parties in 1996.
5. Examples are the green parties that emerged in many European countries in the 1980s (e.g. Müller-Rommel 1989); or the parties of the second Italian republic from 1992 on (e.g. Mershon and Pasquino 1995).
6. See Mair and Mudde (1998) for a useful discussion of the somewhat unwieldy concept of 'party family'.
7. With the accession of Romania and Bulgaria to the EU on 1 January 2007, extreme-right representatives in the EP became numerous enough to form an own parliamentary group. This group dissolved again, however, in November 2007, due to internal splits.
8. See here also Sitter (2002) and Enyedi (2005), who highlight the impact of party (leader) strategy on party system stability and change.
9. See, for example, the special issue of *Comparative Political Studies* (35, no. 8) for an excellent sample of articles on the topic.
10. 'Scepticism' is the *en vogue* term, see Taggart and Szcerbiak (2008).
11. Some of the cited research pieces use complex factor analytical techniques, while others look at bivariate associations. Part of them is based on representative surveys of party voters and party elites, others use party programmes as a source of information, and still others rely on expert judgements on where the parties are (or were at some point in recent history) on a number of issue and ideological dimensions. Some of the survey-based work uses broad summary indicators, while others analyse a multitude of subtle judgements (danger of non-attitudes). All of these differences might have an impact on the findings.

12. Needless to say that this general statement applies in particular in periods of regime change, such as the breakdown of communism in the former Soviet Union and the members of the Warsaw Pact (see e.g. Evans and Whitefield 1998).

13. This is not to deny the possibility of distinguishing a more economic from a more cultural sub-dimension in the overarching left–right dimension. They both contribute — perhaps together with other meaning elements — to the overall meaning of left and right in a given environment.

14. The question wording goes as follows: 'In political matters people talk of "the left" and "the right". What is your position? Please indicate your views using any number on a 10-point-scale. On this scale, where 1 means "left" and 10 means "right", which number best describes your position? ... And about where would you place the following parties on this scale? How about the Labour Party? And ...' Note that in the Swedish study an eleven-point scale (from 0 to 10) was used. We tried to adjust the different scale format by collapsing scale categories '0' and '1' into scale category '1'. The Belgian survey did not ask this question which is why Belgian parties cannot be considered in this analysis.

15. The question wording goes as follows: 'Some say European unification should be pushed further. Others say it already has gone too far. What is your opinion? Please indicate your views using any number on a 10-point-scale. On this scale, 1 means unification "has already gone too far" and 10 means it "should be pushed further". What number on this scale best describes your position? ... And about where would you place the following parties on this scale? How about the Labour Party? And ...' Note that Swedish respondents were asked a different but equivalent question: whether they agree with or oppose Sweden's EU membership, and where they locate the Swedish parties on this scale. Here, again, the Swedish study used an eleven-point scale, which we have tried to adjust as described in the previous footnote.

16. Van der Brug and van der Eijk (1999) have shown that voters' perceptions of party locations are relatively accurate as long as general policy and, in particular, ideological dimensions are concerned. We believe that both the EU dimension and the left–right dimension that are analysed here are of such a general nature and that party positions can be estimated reliably on the basis of representative mass surveys.

17. This frame code identifies to which level of governance a particular argument refers: national, EU or unspecific?

18. The Chappell Hill expert survey used the following question: 'First, we would like you to classify the parties in terms of their broad ideology. On the scale below, 0 indicates that a party is at the extreme left of the ideological spectrum, 10 indicates that it is at the extreme right, and 5 means that it is at the center. For each party, please circle the ideological position that best describes a party's overall ideology'.

19. The Chappell Hill expert survey asked: 'First, how would you describe the general position on European integration that the party's leadership has taken over the course of 2002? For each party row, please circle the number that corresponds best to your view. Circle only one number'. A seven-point answering scale was provided, with the categories strongly opposed, opposed, somewhat opposed, neutral, somewhat in favour, in favour, and strongly in favour.

20. In order to be able to compare directly the findings from three different datasets, the original variables were z-transformed.

21. Note that some of the variation in EP group positions is certainly caused by the fact that the three methods analyse not fully identical samples of EP member parties, that is to say that some parties covered by the voter survey could not be studied in the Euromanifesto analysis, etc.

References

Abendroth, W. 1964. Innerparteiliche und innerverbandliche Demokratie als Voraussetzung der politischen Demokratie. *Politische Vierteljahresschrift* 5: 307–38.

Ágh, A. 1998. *The politics of Central Europe.* London: Sage.

Bakke, E., and N. Sitter. 2005. Patterns of stability: Party competition and strategy in Central Europe since 1989. *Party Politic* 11: 243–63.

Bartolini, S., and P. Mair. 1990. *Identity, competition, and electoral availability. The stabilisation of European electorates 1885–1985.* Cambridge: Cambridge Univ. Press.

Beichelt, T. 2004. Euro-skepticism in the EU accession countries. *Comparative European Politics* 2: 29–50.

Bielasiak, J. 2004. Party systems and EU accession: Euroscepticism in East Europe. Paper presented at the 'Conference on public opinion about the EU in post-communist Eastern Europe', Indiana University, Bloomington, 2–3 April.

Birch, S. 2001. Electoral systems and party system stability in post-communist Europe. Paper presented at the 97th annual meeting of the American Political Science Association, San Francisco, 30 August–2 September.

Bobbio, N. 1996. *Left and right. The significance of a political distinction.* Chicago: Univ. of Chicago Press.

Budge, I., H.-D. Klingemann, A. Volkens, J. Bara, and E. Tannenbaum. 2001. *Mapping policy preferences.* Oxford: Oxford Univ. Press.

Enyedi, Z. 2005. The role of agency in cleavage formation. *European Journal of Political Research* 44: 697–720.

Evans, G., and S. Whitefield. 1998. The evolution of left and right in post-Soviet Russia. *Europe–Asia Studies* 50: 1023–42.

Evans, G., and S. Whitefield. 2000. Explaining the formation of electoral cleavages in post-communist societies. In *Elections in Central and Eastern Europe*, eds. H.-D. Klingemann, E. Mochmann and K. Newton, 36–70. Berlin: Edition Sigma.

Fuchs, D., and H.-D. Klingemann. 1990. The left–right political scheme. In *Continuities in political action*, eds. J. van Deth and M.K. Jennings, 203–34. Berlin: De Gruyter.

Gabel, M., and C.J. Anderson. 2002. The structure of citizen attitudes and the European political space. *Comparative Political Studies* 35: 893–913.

Gabel, M., and S. Hix. 2002. Defining the European political space. An empirical study of the European elections manifestos, 1979–1999. *Comparative Political Studies* 35: 934–64.

Henig, S., ed. 1979. *Political parties in the European Community.* London: George Allan & Unwin.

Hix, S. 2002. A supranational party system and the legitimacy of the European Union. *The International Spectator* 4: 50–9.

Hix, S., and C. Lord. 1997. *Political parties in the European Union.* Houndsmills: Macmillan.

Hix, S., A. Noury, and G. Roland. 2006. *Democratic politics in the European Parliament.* Cambridge: Cambridge Univ. Press.

Hooghe, L., and G. Marks. 2001. *Multi-level governance and European integration.* Lanham, MD: Rowman & Littlefield.

Hooghe, L., G. Marks, and C.J. Wilson. 2002. Does left/right structure party positions on European integration?. *Comparative Political Studies* 35: 965–89.

Kitschelt, H., Z. Mansfeldowa, R. Markowski, and G. Toka. 1999. *Post-communist party systems: Competition, representation, and inter-party cooperation.* Cambridge: Cambridge Univ. Press.

König, Th., E. Rieger, and H. Schmitt, eds. 1996. *Das Europäische Mehrebenensystem — Mannheimer Jahrbuch für Europäische Sozialforschung Bd.1.* Frankfurt: Campus.

Kreppel, A., and G. Gungor. 2004. The institutional integration of an expanded EU or how new European actors fit into old European institutions. Paper presented at the second pan-European conference of the ECPR Standing Group on the European Union, Bologna, 25–6 June.

Kreppel, A., and S. Hix. 2003. From grand coalition to left–right confrontation. *Comparative Political Studies* 36: 75–96.

Laponce, J.A. 1981. *Left and right. The topography of political perceptions.* Toronto: Univ. of Toronto Press.

Lipset, S.M., and S. Rokkan. 1967. Cleavage structures, party systems, and voter alignments: An introduction. In *Party systems and voter alignments*, eds. S.M. Lipset and S. Rokkan, 1–64. New York: Free Press.

Lord, Ch.J. 2006. The aggregating function of political parties in EU decision making. *Living Reviews in European Governance*, http://www.livingreviews.org/lreg-2006-2.

Mair, P., and C. Mudde. 1998. The party family and its study. *Annual Review of Political Science* 1: 211–29.

Marks, G., L. Hooghe, M. Nelson, and E. Edwards. 2006. Party competition and European integration in East and West: Different structure, same causality. *Comparative Political Studies* 39: 155–75.

McElroy, G., and K. Benoit. 2007. Party groups and policy positions in the European Parliament. *Party Politics* 13: 5–28.

Mershon, C., and G. Pasquino, eds. 1995. *Italian politics — Ending the First Republic.* Boulder, CO: Westview.

Müller-Rommel, F. 1989. *New politics in Western Europe: The rise and success of green parties.* Boulder, CO: Westview.

Sartori, G. 1976. *Parties and party systems: A framework for analysis.* Cambridge: Cambridge Univ. Press.

Schmitt, H. 2005. The European Parliament election of June 2004: Still second-order?. *West European Politics* 28: 650–79.

Schmitt, H., and J. Thomassen. 1999. *Political representation and legitimacy in the European Union.* Oxford: Oxford Univ. Press.

Schmitt, H., and J. Thomassen. 2000. Dynamic representation: The case of European integration. *European Union Politics* 1: 319–40.

Sikk, A. 2001. Stabilisation of post-communist party systems. MA diss., University of Tartu.

Sitter, N. 2002. Cleavages, party strategy and party system change in Europe, East and West. *Perspectives on European Politics and Society* 3: 425–51.

Taggart, P., and A. Szcerbiak. 2008. *Opposing Europe. The comparative party politics of Euroscepticism.* 2 vols. Oxford: Oxford Univ. Press.

Thomassen, J., and H. Schmitt. 2004. Democracy and legitimacy in the European Union. *Tidsskrift for Samfunnsforskning* 45, no. 1: 377–410.

Van der Brug, W., and C. Van der Eijk. 1999. The cognitive basis of voting. In *Political representation and legitimacy in the European Union,* eds. H. Schmitt and J. Thomassen. Oxford: Oxford Univ. Press.

Whitefield, S. 2002. Political cleavages and post-communist politics. *Annual Review of Political Science* 5: 181–200.

Whitefield, S., M.A. Vachudova, M. Steenbergen, R. Rohrschneider, G. Marks, M. Loveless, and L. Hooghe. 2006. Do expert survey produce consistent estimates of party stances on European integration?. *Electoral Studies* 26, no. 1: 50–61.

Wüst, A.M., and H. Schmitt. 2007. Comparing the views of parties and voters in the 1999 election to the European Parliament. In *European elections and domestic politics,* eds. W. van der Brug and C. van der Eijk, 73–93. Southbend: Univ. of Notre Dame Press.

The Support Base of Radical Right Parties in the Enlarged European Union

WOUTER VAN DER BRUG & MEINDERT FENNEMA

*Department of Political Science/ASSR, Universiteit van Amsterdam, Amsterdam,
The Netherlands*

ABSTRACT   It was shown on the basis of 1994 data that support for most radical right parties was motivated by the same kind of ideological and pragmatic considerations as support for established parties. On the basis of 1999 data, this was seen to be true only for a small group of successful radical right parties. The current study replicates these analyses on the basis of data from the European Elections Studies 2004. It shows that, by 2004, voters for almost all radical right parties are less motivated by left–right ideology than voters for the established parties. The implications of these results — which are at odds with the literature on niche parties — are discussed.

Introduction

In the last two decades of the twentieth century many Western democracies have seen the rise of parties that have been labelled extreme-right (Ignazi 1992; Hainsworth 2000), New Radical Right (Kitschelt 1995), Radical Right (Norris 2005), right-wing populist (Van der Brug and Mughan 2007) or anti-immigration parties (Fennema 1997). In this paper we study the motives of citizens for supporting these parties. We start from our earlier findings (Van der Brug, Fennema, and Tillie 2000; Van der Brug and Fennema 2003) that the voters for anti-immigrant parties were initially moti-vated by the same ideological and pragmatic considerations as voters for

Correspondence Address: Wouter Van der Brug, Department of Political Science, Universiteit van Amsterdam, Oudezijds Achterburgwal 237, 1012 DL Amsterdam, The Netherlands. E-mail: W.vanderbrug@uva.nl other parties. Analysis of the 1999 European elections, however, showed that this was no longer true for the smaller anti-immigrant parties. We now will analyse the 2004 elections to see whether most voters for anti-immigrant parties are still motivated just as much by considerations that follow the traditional left–right dimension or whether they are driven by other considerations. And, if the latter, what are these specific considerations that drive voters for anti-immigrant parties?

These parties are a mixed bag ideologically. Some of them are inspired directly by fascist intellectuals from the 1930s and speak of the fall of Western civilization (see, for example, Fennema and Pollmann 1998),[1] whereas other such parties have no sympathy at all for the fascist past, and have even criticized the lack of forms of direct democracy in parliamentary democracies. Some have a programme that promotes a free market economy, whereas other such parties have objected against free market arrangements, particularly when it comes to international trade. When Fennema (1997) studied the ideologies of the Western European parties that belong to this group, he concluded that the main thing these parties have in common is their fierce opposition against immigration — the reason why he proposed calling them anti-immigrant parties and, more recently, anti-immigration parties. This term is well suited to describe West-European parties of the radical right. However, if we include parties from central or Eastern Europe the term 'anti-immigration' does not capture what these parties are about. Since immigration into these countries is very limited (apart from former East Germany), these parties have not mobilized against immigrants. Rather, they have promoted strong right-wing nationalism and, as such, they have mobilized anti-EU sentiments, as well as anti-Semitism and hate against other ethnic groups, in particular the Roma (Mudde 2007). So, when looking beyond the context of Western Europe — as we do in this paper — we prefer to use the term radical right (see also Norris 2005).

Until the late 1990s, socio-structural models inspired most research on the radical right. According to this perspective, the rise of radical right parties should be seen as a backlash response to modernization. The crux of these explanations is the suggestion that support for radical right parties comes from citizens who feel threatened by rapid changes in post-industrial societies. Manual workers with low education tend to lose their jobs as a result of changes in modes of production. Moreover, they are competing with immigrant groups for scarce resources, such as jobs and houses. These 'losers of modernity' (Betz 1998a) feel threatened by rapid social change and tend to support radical right-wing parties out of general discontent.

More recent contributions have challenged this perspective that was dominant until the late 1990s. Van der Brug, Fennema, and Tillie (2000) showed that socio-structural characteristics of voters explain less of the variance in support for radical right parties than in support for the more established parties. This means that radical right parties attract their support, more than established parties, across various social boundaries. Moreover, they showed that support for radical right parties is motivated by the same kind of ideological and pragmatic considerations as support for established parties. These analyses were based on 1994 data for seven electoral systems in the EU. A replicating study of 1999 data in eight political systems gave a different picture. For the large and successful radical right parties, such as the FPÖ, Vlaams Blok and Alleanza Nazionale, these conclusions were still valid. However, as regards support for small and unsuccessful radical right parties, such as the Wallonian Front National, the German Republikaner and the Dutch Centrumdemocraten, this was not the case. So, they concluded that two groups of radical right parties have developed in 1999: one group of parties evaluated by their potential supporters on the basis of the same kind of substantive considerations that also motivate support for other parties. We could thus say that citizens treat them as 'normal' parties. The other group of parties is apparently not evaluated on the basis of ideological and pragmatic considerations.

The purpose of the current paper is to replicate the analyses of 1994 and 1999 with data from the European Elections Studies (EES) 2004. This will enable us to assess whether the situation has changed compared to 1999. Moreover, these data enable us to assess the determinants of the vote for three radical right parties that were not included in previous studies: Laos (from Greece), the LPF (from the Netherlands) and the Hungarian Justice and Life Party. In addition to that, the EES 2004 allows us to replicate the findings for six parties that were also included in 1999: the Austrian FPÖ, the Danish Folkepartit, the German Republikaner, the Italian Alleanza Nazionale and Lega Nord, and the French Front Nationale.[2]

What Motivates Voting for Radical Right Parties?

Different kinds of theoretical approaches exist to explain support for radical right parties, as well as differences in aggregate support for such parties. These approaches have looked at the demand-side as well as supply-side factors. In this paper we focus on the motivations of individual voters to support radical right parties, which is why our focus is mainly on the demand side: voters and their grievances and preferences. Different explanations have been put forward.

The first one sees in the resurgence of the market forces, in massive unemployment and in the atomization of a risk society the main cause of the electoral growth of radical right parties. According to this explanation, radical right voting can partially be explained by social isolation. Arendt (1951) was the first to propose this explanation, and others have later found supporting evidence. For instance, Mayer and Moreau (1995) found among the Front National voters and among the voters for the German Republikaner a higher level of social isolation, measured by weak trade union ties and low religious affiliation. Others have, however, argued that community leaders, rather than isolated individuals, decide the fate of the traditional parties and lead the voters to new parties (Hamilton 1982; Martin 1996). It may well be that feelings of social isolation do not stem from social atomization, but rather from a disruption of the traditional relations between local communities and the political power structure. Martin (1996) has stressed the fact that Le Pen voters are found in traditional communities that have lost their lines of communication with the political elites.

In addition to the social isolation thesis, the ethnic competition thesis has been proposed. According to this explanation, support for radical right parties comes from those citizens who feel threatened by rapid changes in post-industrial societies. Blue-collar workers with low education feel insecure because of globalization and immigration. They compete with immigrant groups for scarce resources, such as jobs and houses. These 'losers of modernity' (Betz 1998a) feel threatened by rapid social change and tend to support radical right-wing parties out of resentment against immigrants and against politicians in general, who are held responsible for their uncertainty.

Research has shown that voters who fit Betz' profile — the so-called 'angry white men' — are more likely than other citizens to support radical right parties (e.g. Lubbers 2001; Lubbers, Gijsberts, and Scheepers 2002). However, socio-structural models tend to have very limited power to explain the support of radical right parties (e.g. Van der Brug and Fennema 2003; Norris 2005). Quite the contrary: more than is the case for the established parties, successful radical right parties (such as the Austrian FPÖ in 2000 and the Dutch LPF in 2002) drew their support from all social strata (Van der Brug, Fennema, and Tillie 2000). Recently, Betz (2002) dropped his claims about the 'losers of modernity'.

Another popular explanation of support for radical right parties is the *protest vote* model (Mayer and Perrineau 1992; Betz 1994; Martin 1996; Derks and Deschouwer 1998; Mudde and van Holsteyn 2000; Swyngedouw 2001; Bélanger and Aarts 2006). Unfortunately, however, little conceptual clarity exists about what we mean by the term *protest vote*. Van der Brug, Fennema, and Tillie (2000) conceptualized protest voting as a rational, goal-directed activity. They define protest votes by the motives underlying them. The prime motive behind a protest vote is to show discontent with 'the' political elite. Since radical right parties are treated as outcasts by a large part of the elites in their countries, votes for these parties frighten or shock these elites, which is exactly what the protest voter wants to accomplish (see also Van der Eijk et al. 1996).

In the literature the concept of the 'protest vote' consists of two elements. The first element that distinguishes a protest vote from other types of votes is that discontent with politics (reflected in political cynicism or lack of political trust) should have a strong effect on support for a radical right party (e.g. Van der Brug 2003; Bélanger and Aarts 2006). The second element is, in the words of Lubbers and Scheepers (2000, 69) that 'political attitudes ... are expected to be of minor importance'. The main motivation behind a protest vote is, after all, *not* to affect public policies, but to express discontent (see also Mayer and Perrineau 1992; Kitschelt 1995; Mudde and van Holsteyn 2000).

In previous studies, Van der Brug, Fennema, and Tillie (2000) and Van der Brug and Fennema (2003) rejected the protest vote hypothesis for most of the radical right parties they studied. These studies were criticized for not having direct operationalization of discontent (e.g. Norris 2005) and basing their conclusions instead on indicators of the extent of policy voting for radical right parties. We do not think this critique is warranted. Indeed, the studies did not yield the possibility to demonstrate protest voting if it *had indeed occurred*. However, these studies did show that votes for most radical right parties could not be considered protest votes, because the second element of protest voting (a weak effect of policy preferences) did not apply to them.[3]

Another objection to the conclusions of Van der Brug, Fennema, and Tillie (2000) is that many voters who support radical right parties may combine anti-establishment feelings with substantive policy considerations (e.g. Swyngedouw 2001; Eatwell 2003). While this is certainly true, we are hesitant to use the term *protest vote* for votes that are driven, to a large extent, by substantive policy considerations. If we follow this line of reasoning, we could call votes for any opposition parties protest votes, if these votes are cast by citizens who are relatively discontented. Yet, scholars tend to reserve the term 'protest vote' for those who support radical parties (of the far left or the far right). As a case in point, Bélanger and Aarts (2006) studied the effect of discontent on the vote in the Dutch elections of 2002. It turned out that discontent exerted an almost equally weak (and statistically insignificant) effect on the vote for the radical right LPF as on the Christian Democratic Party, which was the largest opposition party. They interpret this effect — even though it is not significant — as evidence in support of the protest vote hypothesis. Yet they did not answer the question whether Christian Democratic voters should be considered protest voters as well.

We therefore propose to make a qualitative distinction between protest voting and policy voting. In this conceptualization, voters who support a party because they agree with this party on important policy considerations will be called policy voters. Certainly, if these policies are very different from the policies pursued by the government these voters will be discontented. But as long as their vote is driven by these policy considerations, they are policy voters in our definition, no matter how discontented they are. Protest voters on the other hand are voters who support a party out of discontent, but for whom policy considerations are relatively unimportant.

Models of *policy and ideological voting* have not been popular among scholars who study the support for radical right parties, because many researchers find it difficult to believe that voters would vote rationally for what they consider a racist or neo-fascist party. Policy voting models consider voters as rational consumers of policy programmes and political parties as providers of such programmes. In elections several parties provide their policy programmes and voters choose from these alternatives. Of course, voters do not know the content of all these programmes. To be able to choose with restricted information on these programmes, voters rely on other indications of the party programmes. They tend to rely on general information and images that refer to the ideological profile of the parties. The policy voting model predicts therefore that even with limited information the voters' decisions in the ballot box are based on the content of the party programmes (i.e. on issues and ideological positions). Electoral research has shown that votes for many radical right parties — particularly the more successful ones — are predominantly based on policy orientations, which are expressed in left–right positions and attitudes towards immigrants and immigration (Kitschelt 1995; Van der Brug, Fennema, and Tillie 2000; Lubbers, Gijsberts, and Scheepers 2002; Mughan and Paxton 2006; Van der Brug and Fennema 2003). We will now assess to what extent this is still the case in 2004 and whether it is true for the nine radical right parties that we included in this study.

Data and Method

In order to assess whether policy considerations exert a strong or a weak effect on the electoral attractiveness of radical right parties, we must compare the motivations for voting for radical right parties with motivations to vote for other parties. Data from the European Elections Studies provide an excellent opportunity to make this comparison, because the datasets contain comparable information about a large number of parties from all sorts of ideological denominations. For this study we will use data from the European Election Studies 2004, which was conducted immediately following elections to the European Parliament. It consists of cross-sectional surveys using random samples from the electorates of most of the member states of the European Union. In this study we use the surveys from eight countries with one or more parties of the radical right. In Austria 1,010 respondents were interviewed, in Denmark this was 1,317, in France 1,406, in Germany 596, in Greece 500, in Hungary 1,200, in Italy 1,553 and in the Netherlands 1,586. The total sample in these countries thus consists of 9,162 respondents, about 1,145 on average per country.

To compare the motives to support a radical right party with the motives to support other parties we employ a method proposed by Van der Eijk and Franklin (1996). In each country voters were asked, for each party in their political system,[4] how likely it was (on a scale of one to ten) that they would *ever* vote for it. These questions have been carefully designed to yield measures that can be interpreted as the propensity to vote for each of the parties (Van der Eijk and Franklin 1996; Van der Eijk 2002; Van der Eijk et al. 2006). These measures can be regarded for ease of exposition as preferences, but we know that voters make their choice in each election for the party they most prefer.[5]

Having measures of vote propensities serves many purposes, but in this paper the most important function is to provide us with a dependent variable that is comparable across parties (from the same party system, as well as from different party systems): the propensity to vote for a party. When the data matrix is stacked so that each voter appears as many times as there are parties for which her utility has been measured (and other variables have been appropriately transformed as explained below), the question can be posed 'what is it that makes a vote for a party attractive to voters?'. We already know that voters virtually always choose to vote for the party to which they give highest propensity to vote,[6] so an answer to this is also an answer to the question 'what determines which parties are voted for?'. The use of this measure to analyse the determinants of party choice has been validated elsewhere (Tillie 1995; Van der Eijk et al. 2006). There are three conceptual and methodological reasons for using the 'propensity to support' questions as a dependent variable to answer our research questions.

The first reason is that the 'propensity to support' items allow for a research design that is truly comparative (see below). Were we to use party choice as our dependent variable, we would have to conduct separate analyses for each of the countries. Now we can analyse party preference in one single analysis in which all parties from all countries are included. Alternatively, one could do a comparative analysis with a research design proposed by Lubbers, Gijsberts, and Scheepers (2002). They estimated a logistic regression model in which the dependent variable has two values: whether the respondent voted for a radical right party (1) or not (0). This design is not suitable to answer our research question, because it does not allow one to assess whether voters use different criteria to evaluate radical right parties than to evaluate other parties.[7]

Secondly, because some of the radical right-wing parties that we are interested in attract so few votes, estimates of the effects of different variables on decisions to vote for any of these parties are highly unreliable. Since the 'propensity to support' items are asked of all respondents, the parameter estimates are more robust. Finally, if we want to understand the choice process, we cannot afford to look only at the result of that process (the party or candidate voted for), i.e. use party choice as the dependent variable. This is because we lack important information that we need to model this choice process, such as the (differences among) preferences for parties not voted for as well as the preference for the party one did vote for. This information is essential because we know that most voters in Western European countries find more than one party attractive. So, in order to model the motivations underlying the support for radical right parties, we need information about the attractiveness of all parties to all respondents. Since this is what the 'propensity to support' items actually measure, we can analyse the choice process by using these questions as our dependent variable (this argument has been elaborated in more detail elsewhere — see Van der Eijk 2002; Van der Eijk et al. 2006; Van der Brug, Van der Eijk, and Franklin 2007).

The EES 2004 asked this question for nine radical right parties, all mentioned in the introduction, from eight European countries: Austria, Denmark, France, Germany, Greece, Hungary, Italy, and the Netherlands. To assess whether voters evaluate these nine parties by the same criteria as other parties, our study concentrates on the electoral attractiveness of all parties (fifty-eight in total) in the eight political systems included in this study. A valid way to analyse individual and inter-party level variations in party preferences simultaneously can be realized by arranging the data in the so-called 'stacked' (or 'pooled') form first proposed by Stimson (1985) and, after that, applied frequently in electoral research (e.g. MacDonald, Listhaug, and Rabinowitz 1991; Van der Eijk and Franklin 1996; Westholm 1997). In this stacked data matrix each respondent is represented by as many 'cases' as there are parties for which (s)he was asked to indicate the vote propensity. This matrix allows us to apply multiple regression to explain parties' electoral attractiveness. By adding characteristics of the political systems and the parties as variables in the stacked data matrix, such characteristics can be included as variables in these regression analyses. In order to assess whether voting for radical right parties involves a different kind of decision than voting for other parties, we will estimate interaction terms for a radical right party on the one hand, and a set of independent variables on the other. Before getting into this, let us discuss which independent variables are in the equation for predicting parties' electoral attractiveness, and how these are treated in the stacked matrix.

The first predictor of party preference is the subjectively perceived distance between a voter and the respective party in the data matrix on a left–right continuum. Policy voting implies that the closer a party is to someone's own position in terms of policy positions, the more attractive this party will be for the person in question. The questionnaire contained a battery of items in which respondents were asked to indicate their own position as well as that of each political party on a ten-point scale of which the extremes were labelled left and right. These positions are indicative of very general policy preferences. From these responses perceived left–right distances were computed. The stronger the effect of perceived left–right distance on electoral attractiveness, the stronger the extent of ideological voting.

The likelihood of someone voting for radical right parties will also increase when (s)he agrees with the party's stance on some concrete issues (e.g. Billiet and de Witte 1995). EES 2004 contains just one position issue for which respondents' positions and their perceptions of party positions were measured: European integration. This item yields one more predictor of party preference — the perceived distance on this scale between each respondent and the respective party in the data matrix.

Other predictors of party preference are three attitude scales: approval of the current national government, approval of the European Union and satisfaction with the way democracy works. The latter is not regularly included in models of party choice, but since the paper investigates radical right parties that are sometimes critical of parliamentary democracies, we included this measure. The survey also contained the question 'what is the most important problem facing the country?' The responses were coded in categories, and we created dummy variables, one for each of the categories. These were used to assess the influence of political priorities on party preferences.

In addition to these attitude scales, we included a number of socio-structural and demographic variables in the model: social class, education, gender, religion and age. Class is measured with a variable asking for the respondent's subjective idea of his/her social class. Religion is a composite variable of religious denomination and church attendance.

Creating the stacked data matrix produces a dependent variable, 'party preference', which is generic in the sense of having no party-specific meaning. The problem here, though, is that the relationship between dependent and independent variables is usually directionally specific. For example, church attendance can be expected to have a negative effect on support for a liberal party and a positive one on that for a Christian Democratic Party. In the case of the effect of left–right ideology, this directionality problem could be overcome easily when computing the ideological distance between each party and each respondent. This was not the case for the socio-structural and the attitude scales, however, since the surveys do not contain matching party characteristics for them. In order, therefore, to create generic independent variables that can be 'stacked on top of each other', we adopted a procedure that involves the linear transformation of the original socio-structural and issue variables (see, for example, Van der Eijk and Franklin 1996; Van der Brug, Van der Eijk, and Franklin 2007). One outcome of this transformation of some of the predictor variables is that their influence will *always be positive*.[8]

Finally, we included a variable at the party level, *party size*, which represents a strategic consideration that voters may take into account: when two parties are about equally attractive on all relevant accounts, voters tend to vote for the largest one because it stands a better chance of achieving its policy goals. We called this type of voting 'pragmatic'. Party size is measured by each parties' proportion of seats in parliament.

In a number of subsequent steps we will assess to what extent support of radical right parties is determined by particular considerations that exert less (or no) effect on support of other parties. These party-specific considerations are detected in the following way. First, we will start with an estimation of the regression model on the stacked matrix that includes all fifty-eight parties. Also, we will do the same for the subgroup of nine radical right parties, and for the forty-nine other parties. These analyses will allow only for an *ad oculum* comparison of differences in the effect parameters. As a final step we will therefore explore whether significant interaction effects exist between each of the radical right parties on the one hand and various predictors of party preference on the other. This will be done for the model that was estimated for the total of fifty-eight parties. Such interaction effects, were they to exist, would indicate that support of radical right parties is determined by *party-specific* factors. If we cannot find such interaction effects, or if they turn out to be very small, then we will have to conclude that voters treat radical right parties just like any other party.[9]

Results

Table 1 presents the results of three regression analyses. In the first one the model is estimated for all fifty-eight parties, in the second one only the nine radical right parties are included, and the third analysis includes the forty-nine other parties. In the analyses of all fifty-eight parties a (dummy) variable was included that distinguishes the nine radical right parties from the forty-nine others. The regression coefficient for this variable tells us whether any differences exist between the electoral attractiveness of radical right parties on the one hand and 'mainstream' parties on the other, after controlling for the effects of the other independent variables. In other words, the coefficient tells us whether — after we take the effects of social characteristics, policy preferences, etc. into account — radical right parties are considered more or less attractive than other parties. Here the findings are somewhat different from those in 1994 and 1999 (see Van der Brug, Fennema, and Tillie 2000; Van der Brug and Fennema 2003). In those years the dummy variable that distinguishes radical right parties from mainstream parties turned out to yield the only parameter in the equation that did not deviate significantly from zero. However, in 2004 and for the selection of parties included here, the dummy variable for radical right parties is negative and significant. This means that, after all factors that affect preferences for parties have been taken into account, preferences for radical right parties are still, on average, lower than preferences for other parties (0.65 units on a ten-point scale).

Because different issues are included in the European Elections Studies of 1994, 1999 and 2004, the results presented in Table 1 are not fully comparable to those in previous studies. However, a few general remarks can be made about the model that we tested for fifty-eight parties. Judging by the magnitude of the standardized coefficients, in all three years the left–right distance between parties and voters is the strongest determinant of electoral preferences. The significance of the left–right dimension for structuring the behaviour of voters has been observed by many scholars (e.g. Fuchs and Klingemann 1990; Van der Eijk and Franklin 1996; Hix 1999; Schmitt 2001).

Another stable finding is that *party size* is the variable with the second strongest effect on party preference. The positive effect of party size shows that, after controlling for policy positions and social characteristics, voters consider a larger party more attractive than a smaller one. Voters who wish to influence policy making take into account the strategic consideration that a large party has a better chance than a smaller one to realize its policy goals. So, electoral preferences are determined by a combination of *ideological* and *pragmatic* considerations.

The magnitude of the effects of socio-structural variables, issue priorities and attitudes towards the EU, is also remarkably stable. In comparison to the other years, there is only one major difference. Government approval has a substantively stronger effect in 2004 than it had in the other election years. In 1999, the standardized effect of government approval was 0.09, whereas in 2004 it is 0.22. Compared to the other years, voters tend to base their electoral preferences more than in previous years on their evaluation of the performance of parties in government. Since this is beyond the scope of this paper, we will not explore this matter further here.

How does this general model compare to the model for the nine radical right parties? The most important conclusion of Table 1 is that most of the effects are quite similar in magnitude. Note that as a result of the linear transformations of most of the independent variables, those parameters are necessarily positive, so that no conclusions can be drawn about the direction of the effects. Socio-structural and demographic characteristics — gender, age, religion, social class and education — have almost the same weak effect

Table 1. Regressions of full models for the explanation of part support in eight countries

	All 58 parties			9 radical right parties			49 established parties		
	b	SE	Beta	b	SE	Beta	b	SE	Beta
Social class	0.558	0.037	0.075**	0.681	0.126	0.077**	0.544	0.039	0.076**
Religion	0.625	0.034	0.115**	0.813	0.104	0.111**	0.607	0.033	0.117**
Gender	0.675	0.120	0.035**	0.951	0.182	0.060**	0.645	0.133	0.033**
Education	0.509	0.051	0.056**	0.456	0.117	0.047**	0.516	0.055	0.059**
Age	0.414	0.058	0.041**	0.956	0.330	0.028*	0.397	0.059	0.043**
Importance of issues	0.619	0.045	0.076**	0.696	0.090	0.111**	0.608	0.050	0.074**
EU approval	0.503	0.045	0.065**	0.676	0.095	0.102**	0.472	0.049	0.061**
Government approval	0.655	0.019	0.223**	0.597	0.047	0.141**	0.649	0.020	0.232**
Satisfaction with democracy	0.335	0.040	0.045**	0.574	0.086	0.077**	0.311	0.044	0.043**
Perceived distance European unification	−0.060	0.009	−0.044**	−0.062	0.013	−0.064**	−0.060	0.010	−0.042**
Perceived distance on left–right	−0.373	0.009	−0.286**	−0.255	0.013	−0.262**	−0.402	0.010	−0.296**
Radical right party (dummy variable)	−0.651	0.037	−0.015**						
Party size	4.353	0.089	0.221**	6.133	0.528	0.134**	4.301	0.089	0.248**
R²-adjusted		0.365			0.255			0.353	
Number of clusters (respondents)		7,470			7,274			7,461	
Number of units of analysis		56,080			8,358			47,722	

*significant at $p<0.01$; **significant at $p<0.001$.

on electoral preferences for radical right parties as on electoral preferences for other parties. Also, the effect of left–right distance on electoral preferences is very similar for the two groups of parties.

Judging by the standardized coefficients, two variables exert weaker effects. The first one is party size, but this difference may be caused by the fact that the variation in party size is substantially smaller among the radical right parties than among the other parties. Note also that the unstandardized coefficient is higher, so that we have to be particularly careful when comparing these effects across different equations. The other effect that is substantially weaker among radical right parties than among other parties is approval of the government. The most likely explanation for this weaker effect is that there are relatively few government parties among the radical right parties, and that this variable has a particularly strong effect on electoral preferences for government parties. We may conclude, however, that support of radical right parties is not determined strongly by dissatisfaction with the government.

In contrast to what one might expect *a priori* on the basis of the nationalist ideologies of parties of the radical right, the issue of European integration exerts an effect on preferences for radical right-wing parties that is very similar to its effect on preferences for other parties. The same goes for citizens' satisfaction with the EU and satisfaction with the way democracy functions. Despite the anti-parliamentarian rhetoric of these parties, dissatisfaction with democracy is not an important motivation for citizens to support these types of parties.

Negative attitudes towards immigrants are an important predictor of the vote for radical right parties (e.g. Lubbers, Gijsberts, and Scheepers 2002; Van der Brug and Fennema 2003; Norris 2005). The EES of 2004 does not contain measures of attitudes towards immigrants, so that the effect of this issue cannot be tested. In many countries this issue will be incorporated in the left–right dimension, so to some extent the strong effect of left–right distances reflects the effect attitudes towards immigrants, but the explained variance of the model would certainly have been higher if these attitudes had been measured.

A final important observation is that socio-structural and demographic variables exert only very weak effects on electoral preferences for radical right and for the other parties. Various scholars have observed that cleavage politics is declining in most countries and that this decline is largely compensated for by an increase in policy voting (Franklin 1992, 400). Instead of relying on social positions as a 'cue' to decide which party to vote for, the increasingly autonomous citizens vote largely on the basis of their policy preferences (e.g. Rose and McAllister 1986; Dalton 1996). Our results show that this is just as true of supporters of radical right parties as it is of voters for other parties. Radical right parties do not attract the 'losers of modernity' as Betz used to call them, but they attract their supporters across all social strata.

The comparisons between electoral preferences for various radical right parties and other parties have so far been made for all nine parties of the radical right together, and on an *ad oculum* basis. The design of our analyses, with a stacked data matrix in which electoral preferences are studied for all parties simultaneously, provides the opportunity to systematically study differences among the radical right-wing parties, and, also between radical right-wing parties and other parties. If a variable has a different effect for one party than for all other parties, the regression model should contain an interaction term between the respective party on the one hand and this variable on the other.

To estimate these interactions, we estimated two models. The first model is the model in Table 1 estimated for all fifty-eight parties with three interactions added to the model: interactions between on the one hand a dummy variable that separates the nine radical right parties from the other forty-nine and, on the other hand, party size, left–right distance and distance on the issue of European unification.[10] Model 1 in Table 2 presents the parameter estimates of these interaction terms as well as the main effects of party size, left–right distance and distance on European unification. The models also included the effects of the other independent variables presented in Table 1, but these are not shown because in order to assess whether the determinants of support for radical right parties is different from the determinants of support for other parties, we are interested only in the interaction effects.

The analysis with one dummy variable for the nine radical right parties together, yields significant positive interaction effects for left–right distance and for party size. To interpret these interaction effects they have to be compared to the main effects. The main effect from left–right distance on electoral attractiveness (for all parties) is −0.401. This negative effect is as expected: the larger the ideological distance the less attractive is a party. The positive interaction effect of left–right distance shows that the negative

Table 2.   Interactions with radical right parties

		Ideological distance (left–right)	Distance European unification	Party size
Model 1	Main effects	−0.401**	−0.059**	4.309**
	9 radical right parties	0.148**	−0.011	1.510*
Model 2	Main effects	−0.401**	−0.059**	4.309**
	FPÖ	0.149**	−0.035	–
	Dansk Folkeparti	0.068	−0.135**	–
	FN (French)	0.120**	−0.020	–
	Republikaner	0.253**	0.027	–
	LAOS	0.190**	0.014	–
	Alleanza Nazionale	−0.065	0.032	–
	Lega Nord	0.148**	−0.055	–
	LPF	0.073*	−0.016	–
	Justice and Life	0.193**	0.025	–

*significant at $p<0.01$; **significant at $p<0.001$.
Source: European Elections Study 2004.

effect of left–right distance is somewhat weaker for radical right-wing parties than for the other parties: the unstandardized effect for radical right parties is –0.252 (–0.401 + 0.148). The positive interaction effect of [party size * radical right] in Table 2 shows that the effect of party size is somewhat stronger for radical right-wing parties than for other parties. We should, however, take into account that the radical right parties in our sample tend to be relatively small parties. So, the larger effect could be indicative of certain threshold effects for small parties, as a result of which small parties may benefit more from becoming larger than large parties. The third interaction term, the one for European unification, turns out not to be statistically significant. So, this issue has the same weak effect on preferences for radical right parties as on preferences for other parties. In other words, anti-EU feelings hardly contribute to support for the radical right.

In the second model we look at all nine radical right parties separately. So, instead of a dummy variable for the nine radical right parties, we added nine dummies for each one of them. And we added the interactions between these dummy variables and distances on left–right and on European unification. The relevant results of this model (Model 2) are presented in the lower half of Table 2.

Our findings for 2004 have so far largely confirmed the findings of 1999. However, when we inspect the differences among the various parties of the radical right, we must conclude that things are quite different in 2004 than they were in 1999 and considerably different than in 1994. In 1994 there was only one single party — the Dutch Centrumdemocraten — for which we found weaker effects of left–right ideology. In 1999 there were more parties for which this was the case: the effect of left–right distance was significantly weaker for the Centrumdemocraten, the Wallonian Front National, the German Republikaner, the Lega Nord, the French Front national and the Danish Fremskridtpartiet. In that year there were four exceptions, which were the four most successful radical right parties: the FPÖ, Alleanza Nazionale, Vlaams Blok and Dansk Folkeparti. Their support was at least as heavily determined by ideology as votes for other parties. Even though a comparison over time is hindered by the different selections of parties, the results of 2004 suggest that the trend seems to have continued. The effect of left–right distance is significantly weaker for seven radical right parties (the German Republikaner, the Italian Lega Nord, the French Front National, the Dutch LPF, the Greek Laos, the Hungarian party for Justice and Life, and the Dutch LPF) than it is for other parties. Only for two parties, the Danish FP and the Italian AN, are the effects of the same magnitude. So, it appears that the effect of left–right distances on electoral support for radical right parties has declined overall since 1994.

Conclusion and Discussion

In terms of how they attract votes, are radical right parties different from other parties? In the analyses we focused on the differences and, indeed, we found important differences between radical right parties and other parties.

The most important difference is that the effect of left–right tends to be weaker. However, when focusing on these differences we tend to overlook the large similarities.

A first similarity between the processes that generate support for radical right-wing parties and processes generating support for other parties is that the effects of socio-structural variables are weak. This means that radical right-wing parties, like most other parties, attract their support from across all different strata in society. Secondly, left–right distance is the strongest predictor of support for radical right parties as well as other parties, even though the effect is weaker for the former than the latter. Thirdly, the effect of party size is at least as important for radical right parties as it is for other parties, so that we may conclude that the pragmatic consideration that a larger party is more attractive than a smaller one, because it is in a better position to affect public policies or to be heard in the public debate, is just as important to voters when judging a radical right party as it is when judging other parties (see also Bos and Van der Brug, forthcoming). Finally, neither dissatisfaction with the functioning of democracy, nor dissatisfaction with European unification, nor dissatisfaction with the government exerts a strong effect on support for radical right parties. Because of all these similarities, we should be careful not to think of supporters of radical right parties as the 'losers of modernity', as Betz (1994) used to call them, who support these parties to express general feelings of discontent.

On the other hand, our analyses have revealed large changes since Van der Brug, Fennema, and Tillie (2000) concluded on the basis of the 1994 EES data that there were hardly any differences between the determinants of support for radical right parties and the determinants of votes for other parties. The main difference is nowadays that the effect of left–right is weaker. This is at odds with some of the literature on niche parties (e.g. Meguid 2005), alternatively called 'fringe parties'. According to Meguid (2005), niche parties enter the electoral arena by mobilizing support on new issues that are not integrated in the dominant dimensions of conflict (i.e. left–right). When such parties are successful, mainstream parties respond either by contrasting their positions on the new issue with that of the niche party or by co-opting. In both cases the new issue would become more integrated in the existing cleavage lines. Even though Meguid does not make predictions about the effect of left–right on the vote, one would expect on the basis of this pattern that the effect of left–right on support for niche parties would become stronger over time rather than weaker. Since these new parties mobilize support on new issues, voters have difficulties evaluating new parties on the basis of their ideological leaning on the left–right dimension. When niche parties become more familiar to voters, and when 'their' issue becomes more integrated in the left–right dimension, voters will evaluate them in these terms (see also Tillie 1995; Van der Brug, Franklin, and Toka 2008). This process, which has been detected in the early phase of the life-cycle of anti-immigrant parties (see Tillie and Fennema 1998), seems to have reversed after 1994. So, why do voters in 2004 no longer evaluate these parties as much by their left–right position as they used to?

A possible explanation could be that many of these parties strongly evaluated in left–right terms in 1994, such as the FPÖ, the Republikaner, and Front National, have lost much of their credibility as a result of poor performance as government parties (FPÖ), and internal party conflicts (all of these three). In addition, mainstream right parties in many countries have co-opted the anti-immigration positions of the radical right to some extent. It is conceivable that the single issue character of these latter parties hence became more evident and more problematic when their prime issues were co-opted. Even though some of them have tried to elaborate their ideological positions outside the domain of immigration and integration, most of them remain to be seen as anti-immigrant parties. We expect the effect of left–right to be weaker for single-issue parties than for parties with a broader ideological profile, because left–right is a generic ideological dimension. Moreover, when these parties have lost their 'unique selling proposition' to some extent because the mainstream right co-opts their core issues, the protest character of these parties may also become more visible.

Some parties resist this trend and are still strongly evaluated according to the left–right dimension. These parties have managed to be seen as 'normal parties'. They have either been members of a coalition government (AN) or have passively supported a government (DFP), without creating internal party struggles. As such they have been able to promote the further restriction of immigration,[11] but they are still evaluated in generic terms, not only in connection with the issue of immigration. The Dansk Folkepartit and Alleanza Nazionale have managed to build up a good functioning party organization. This may be key to their sustained electoral success, as has been suggested also for the Flemish Vlaams Blok, renamed Vlaams Belang (see also Mudde 2007).

This brings us to a final point: are these parties here to stay? Previous studies have shown that these parties have mobilized support largely on the basis of anti-immigration sentiments, so that the continued success of these parties depends on the saliency of this issue. Over past decades the immigration issue has become a rather stable theme for party political contestation in many established democracies (e.g. Kriesi et al. 2008; Van der Brug and van Spanje 2009). Whether this issue is 'owned' by radical right parties or whether the issue is incorporated by the mainstream parties depends on the discursive and political opportunity structures for radical right parties. Still, even during the financial crisis that began in 2008, anti-immigration parties have managed to do well in the polls. We would therefore expect that in most Western European countries these parties will continue to be important 'players'.

Notes

1. Some even used 1930s jargon, such as the 'fall of the Occident'.
2. Unfortunately, we cannot include Vlaams Blok from Flanders, Front Nationale from Wallonia, New Democracy from Sweden, the British National Party from Britain and the National Party from Poland, because the relevant variables are missing.
3. For some smaller radical right parties, such as the Dutch Centrumdemocraten, these studies found only very weak effects of policy preferences. This could mean that the supporters of such

parties were indeed protest voters, but in the absence of indicators of discontent, this cannot be established.
4. In practice, the parties asked about included only those with representation in the national parliament or those widely expected to obtain representation in the European Parliament.
5. In practice this occurs about 93 per cent of the time in established EU member states.
6. See note 5.
7. Moreover, a dependent variable that distinguishes only between radical right and other parties does not realistically reflect the electoral process.
8. Except for odd cases where statistically insignificant effects can become negative in multivariate models.
9. Conceptually one could argue that each radical right party should be compared only to the other parties in the same party system. However, that would preclude us from testing the effects of party characteristics, such as party size, since such variables become constants when focusing on single parties within a country. Comparing the effects for radical right parties to such effects for all other parties is warranted, because prior research showed that the causal mechanisms behind party choice are very similar across very different European countries (e.g. Van der Eijk and Franklin 1996; Van der Brug, Franklin, and Toka 2008).
10. The method does not allow us to estimate interaction effects for the other variables in the model. The reason is that their effects were originally estimated with a procedure that involves a linear transformation of the original variables. This procedure provides a valid way to estimate the strength of each of the independent variables, but at the same time rules out the possibility to estimate interaction effects. As the topic of this paper focuses primarily on the effect of party size and left–right distance (two variables that were not transformed) we do not consider this to be a problem here.
11. The position of Alleanza Nazionale on this issue is diffuse. AN's leader Fini was, as a minister, responsible for the Bossi-Fini law to restrict immigration, but he also supported a proposal to grant the right to vote in municipal elections to legal immigrants in Italy. Apparently, AN is an anti-immigration party, but not an anti-immigrant party.

References

Arendt, H. 1951. *The origins of totalitarianism.* Orlando: Harcourt Brace & Company.
Bélanger, E., and K. Aarts. 2006. Explaining the rise of the LPF: Issues, discontent, and the 2002 Dutch elections. *Acta Politica*: 4–20.
Betz, H-G. 1994. *Radical right-wing populism in Western Europe.* Basingstoke: Macmillan.
Betz, H-G. 1998a. Introduction. In Betz and Immerfall 1998, 1–10.
Betz, H-G. 1998b. Against Rome: The Lega Nord. In Betz and Immerfall 1998, 45–58.
Betz, H-G. 2002. Rechtspopulismus und Rechtsradikalismus in Europa. *Österreichische Zeitschrift für Politikwissenschaft* 2003/2: 251–64.
Betz, H-G., and S. Immerfall. 1998. *The new politics of the right: Neo-populist parties and movements in established democracies.* Basingstoke: Macmillan.
Billiet, J., and H. de Witte. 1995. Attitudinal dispositions to vote for a 'new' extreme right-wing party: The case of 'Vlaams Blok'. *European Journal of Political Research* 27, no. 2: 181–202.
Bos, L., and W. Van der Brug. Forthcoming. Public images of leaders of anti-immigration parties. *Party Politics.*
Dalton, R.J. 1996. *Citizen politics in Western democracies; Public opinion and political parties in advanced industrial democracies.* Chatham: Chatham House.
Derks, A., and K. Deschouwer. 1998. Vrijzinnigen, ongelovigen en protest. In *Kiezen is verliezen. Onderzoek naar de politieke opvattingen van Vlamingen,* eds. Marc Swyngedouw, Jaak Billiet, Ann Carton and Roeland Beerten, 85–112. Leuven/Amersfoort: Acco.
Eatwell, Roger. 1998. The dynamics of right-wing electoral breakthrough. *Patterns of Prejudice* 32: 1–31.
Eatwell, Roger. 2003. Ten theories of the extreme right. In *Right-wing extremism in the twenty-first century,* eds. Peter Merkl and L. Weinberg. London: Frank Cass.
Fennema, M. 1997. Some conceptual issues and problems in the comparison of anti-immigrant parties in Western Europe. *Party Politics* 3: 473–92.

Fennema, M., and C. Pollmann. 1998. Ideology of anti-immigrant parties in the European Parliament. *Acta Politica* 33: 111–38.

Franklin, M. 1992. The decline of cleavage politics. In *Electoral change. Responses to evolving social and attitudinal structures in Western countries,* eds. M. Franklin, T. Mackie and H. Valen, 383–405. Cambridge: Cambridge Univ. Press.

Fuchs, D., and H.D. Klingemann. 1990. The left–right scheme: Theoretical framework. In *Continuities in political action: A longitudinal study of political orientations in three Western democracies,* eds. M.K. Jennings and J. van Deth, 203–34. Berlin: De Gruyter.

Hainsworth, Paul, ed. 2000. *The politics of the extreme right: From the margins to the mainstream.* London: Pinter.

Hamilton, R.F. 1982. *Who voted for Hitler?.* Princeton: Princeton Univ. Press.

Hix, S. 1999. Dimensions and alignments in European Union politics: Cognitive constraints and partisan responses. *European Journal of Political Research* 35: 69–106.

Ignazi, P. 1992. The silent counter-revolution: Hypotheses on the emergence of extreme right-wing parties in Europe. *European Journal of Political Research* 22, no. 1: 3–34.

Kitschelt, H. 1995. *The radical right in Western Europe. A comparative analysis.* Ann Arbor: Univ. of Michigan Press.

Kriesi, Hanspeter, Edgar Grande, Romain Lachat, Martin Dolezal, Simon Bornschier, and Timotheos Frey. 2008. *West European politics in the age of globalization.* Cambridge: Cambridge Univ. Press.

Lubbers, M. 2001. Exclusionistic electorates. Extreme right-wing voting in Western Europe. PhD diss., Nijmegen ICS.

Lubbers, M., M. Gijsberts, and P. Scheepers. 2002. Extreme right-wing voting in Western Europe. *European Journal of Political Research* 41: 345–78.

Lubbers, M., and P. Scheepers. 2000. Individual and contextual characteristics of the German extreme right vote in the 1990s. *European Journal of Political Research* 38, no. 1: 63–94.

Macdonald, S.E., O. Listhaug, and G. Rabinowitz. 1991. Issues and party support in multiparty systems. *American Political Science Review* 85: 1107–31.

Martin, P. 1996. Le vote Le Pen. L'électorat du Front national. *Notes de la fondation Saint-Simon,* October/November 1996, Paris.

Mayer, N., and P. Moreau. 1995. Electoral support for the German Republikaner and the French National Front 1989–1994. Paper presented at the Workshop on Racist Parties in Europe of the ECPR Joint Sessions of Workshops, 27 April–2 May, Bordeaux.

Mayer, N., and P. Perrineau. 1992. Why do they vote for Le Pen?. *European Journal of Political Research* 22, no. 1: 123–41.

Meguid, B.M. 2005. Competition between unequals: The role of mainstream party strategy in niche party success. *American Political Science Review* 99: 347–59.

Mudde, C. 2007. *Populist radical right parties in Europe.* Cambridge: Cambridge Univ. Press.

Mudde, C., and J. van Holsteyn. 2000. The Netherlands: Explaining the limited success of the extreme right. In Hainsworth 2000, 144–71.

Mughan, A., and P. Paxton. 2006. Anti-immigrant sentiment, policy preferences and populist party voting in Australia. *British Journal of Political Science* 36, no. 2: 341–58.

Norris, Pippa. 2005. *Radical right. Voters and parties in the electoral market.* New York: Cambridge Univ. Press.

Rogers, W.H. 1993. Regression standard errors in clustered samples. *Stata Technical Bulletin* 13: 19–23.

Rose, R., and I. McAllister. 1986. *Voters begin to choose.* Beverly Hills: Sage.

Schmitt, H. 2001. *Politische Repräsentation in Europa.* Frankfurt: Campus.

Stimson, J.A. 1985. Regression in space and time: A statistical essay. *American Journal of Political Science* 29: 914–47.

Swyngedouw, M. 2001. The subjective cognitive and affective map of extreme right voters: Using open-ended questions in exit polls. *Electoral Studies* 20: 217–41.

Tillie, J. 1995. *Party utility and voting behaviour.* Amsterdam: Het Spinhuis.

Tillie, J., and M. Fennema. 1998. A rational choice for the extreme right. *Acta Politica* 34: 223–49.

Van der Brug, W. 2003. How the LPF fuelled discontent: Empirical tests of explanations of LPF-support. *Acta Politica. International Journal of Political Science* 38, no. 1: 89–106.

Van der Brug, W., and M. Fennema. 2003. Protest or mainstream? How the European anti-immigrant parties have developed into two separate groups by 1999. *European Journal of Political Research* 42, no. 1: 55–76.

Van der Brug, W., M. Fennema, and J. Tillie. 2000. Anti-immigrant parties in Europe: Ideological or protest vote?. *European Journal of Political Research* 37: 77–102.

Van der Brug, W., M. Franklin, and G. Toka. 2008. One electorate or many? Differences in party preference formation between new and established European democracies. *Electoral Studies* 27, no. 4: 589–600.

Van der Brug, W., and A. Mughan. 2007. Charisma, leader effects and support for right-wing populist parties. *Party Politics* 13, no. 1: 29–51.

Van der Brug, W., C. Van der Eijk, and M. Franklin. 2007. *The economy and the vote: Economic conditions and elections in fifteen countries.* Cambridge: Cambridge Univ. Press.

Van der Brug, W., and J. van Spanje. 2009. Immigration, Europe and the 'new' cultural cleavage. *European Journal of Political Research* 48: 309–34.

Van der Eijk, C. 2002. Design issues in electoral research: Taking care of (core) business. *Electoral Studies* 21: 189–206.

Van der Eijk, C., and M. Franklin. 1996. *Choosing Europe? The European electorate and national politics in the face of union.* Ann Arbor: Univ. of Michigan Press.

Van der Eijk, C., M. Franklin, and M. Marsh. 1996. What voters teach us about European elections/ what European elections teach us about voters. *Electoral Studies* 15: 149–66.

Van der Eijk, C., M. Franklin, and H. Schmitt. 1999. *European Elections Study 1999: Design, implementation and results.* Colgne: Zentralarchiv für Emprische Sozialforschung.

Van der Eijk, C., M. Franklin, and W. Van der Brug. 1999. Policy preferences and party choice. In *Political representation and legitimacy in the European Union*, eds. H. Schmitt and J. Thomassen, 161–85. Oxford: Oxford Univ. Press.

Van der Eijk, C., W. Van der Brug, M. Kroh, and M. Franklin. 2006. Rethinking the dependent variable in electoral behavior — On the measurement and analysis of utilities. *Electoral Studies* 25, no. 3: 424–47.

Westholm, A. 1997. Distance versus direction: The illusory defeat of the proximity theory of electoral choice. *American Political Science Review* 91: 865–83.

Williams, R.L. 2000. A note on robust variance estimation for cluster-correlated data. *Biometrics* 56, no. 3: 645–46.

Appendix A

The stacked matrix, combining party preferences for the fifty-eight parties from eight political systems has a total of 56,080 units of analysis, after deletion of missing cases in the dependent variable. To estimate the parameters of the regression models, units of analyses are weighted in two steps. As a result of the weight factor applied in the first step respondents in each system are weighted in such a way that their party choice in the European Elections 2004 reflects exactly the actual election results. In the second step this weight variable is multiplied by a (different) constant for each system, so that the eight systems in the stacked matrix contain the same number of cases. This weight variable was used for the analyses in which all parties from the eight different political systems are analysed simultaneously. Each time groups of parties are selected, the variable generated in the first stage is multiplied by yet different constants for each system, so that in all regressions presented in Table 1 the eight systems in the stacked matrix contain the same number of units of analysis each.

Because we stacked the data, the unit of analysis is no longer the individual respondent, but the respondent/party combination. Since these are not independent observations, we computed panel-corrected standard errors, and reported significance on the basis of these tests. To be precise, we did these analyses in STATA, using the robust estimate of variance (known as the Huber/White/Sandwich estimate of variance) and the 'cluster' option to adjust for the dependency among observations pertaining to the same respondent (Rogers 1993; Williams 2000). Each of the 7,470 respondents was defined as a separate cluster.

Turning Out or Turning Off: Do Mobilization and Attitudes Account for Turnout Differences between New and Established Member States at the 2004 EP Elections?

BERNHARD WESSELS* & MARK N. FRANKLIN**

*Social Science Research Center Berlin (WZB), Research Unit 'Democracy: Structures, Performance, Challenges', Berlin, Germany; **Department of Political and Social Science, European University Institute, Florence, Italy

ABSTRACT How can we understand the low turnout seen in the 2004 European Parliament elections? One possibility would be that new member states were 'just different' either because of the post-communist legacy in some of them or because of an unexplicated 'low propensity to vote' in some of those. This article explicates the low propensity to vote in some post-communist countries by means of a general model of turnout that applies also to established EU member states. In this model low turnout is accounted for by party loyalties on the one hand, and affective and instrumental reasons for voting on the other. The latter factors are found to be lacking in European Parliament elections, which can nevertheless see high turnout due to party loyalty or compulsory voting. Where both of these are absent we see particularly low turnout, as we did in five of the new member countries in 2004.

Introduction

Since the first European Parliament elections in 1979, turnout has been in decline. This is just the opposite of what one would expect from the increasing

Correspondence Address: Bernhard Wessels, Social Science Research Center Berlin (WZB), Research Unit 'Democracy: Structures, Performance, Challenges', Reichpietschufer 50, 10785 Berlin, Germany. E-mail: wessels@wzb.eu relevance of the European Union as a more and more powerful political system and the increasing significance of the European Parliament within this system.

The decline in turnout has raised many questions and worries. Whereas the level of turnout compared across countries may not signify political satisfaction where it is high, nor the opposite where it is low, decline across time certainly does indicate that something is going on. Mark Franklin (2001) demonstrated the strong impact of the composition of the EU as new countries were admitted to membership and the additional importance of demographic change in the composition of the eligible population by lowered voting age (Franklin 2004). But the European Parliament elections of 2004 gave rise to a further fall in turnout that goes beyond anything that can be explained readily in such terms.

The 2004 European elections were indeed an event whose historical importance can be barely overstated. That enlargement of the EU moved the borders of the community far to the east of the former Iron Curtain. The 2004 EP elections can be called the 'founding elections' of the new Europe, overcoming the obsolete East–West divide. It was the first opportunity for the sovereign peoples in the East to express their belonging and indicate their preferences for the political course of the Union. And, it was a chance for the people in the old member states to demonstrate the historical significance of the event by participating in it.

None of this happened. Turnout was, on average, extremely low in the new member states, and even in the old member states it was a little lower than in 1999. Richard Rose (2004) points out that the low turnout was a feature not of new member states but of post-communist new members. His explanation for the low turnout in these countries was lack of trust in political parties and governments, legacies of communist rule. This suggestion seems somewhat quixotic, however. Political trust has not been found previously to be related to turnout in EP elections and its influence in certain studies of national turnout has been shown to be due to the use of underspecified models (Franklin 2004). Indeed, Rose's suggestion that we distinguish post-communist states from others seems to miss the mark. Not all of the post-communist member states displayed particularly low turnout in the 2004 EP elections. In Lithuania turnout was 48 per cent, about average for non-communist member states and, in Hungary and Latvia, turnout was 39 and 41 per cent, no lower than in Britain, Finland or Sweden. If all post-communist EU member states had displayed turnout in this range, no one would have remarked upon the supposed low turnout of these countries. Several West European countries had specific reasons for higher turnout that did not apply in the post-communist states.

So what does account for turnout among low-turnout EU member states? This question has two sides. In the first place we need to know whether citizens of these countries respond to the same institutional and contextual influences as citizens of established member states. To evaluate this question, we apply a 'standard model' introduced by Franklin (2001, 2005). Because this model fails to explain the differences we see between low-turnout countries and others, an information-mobilization approach and an attitudinal approach are developed to address two differences — political community and evaluation of the EU political system — that we observe to exist between different EU member states. Overall in this paper, four sets of hypotheses are tested:

- *'Standard model' hypothesis.* Aggregate turnout is a product of compulsory voting, time until next national election, and first election boost (Franklin 2001, 2005). The latter two aspects relate to mobilization. The mobilization hypothesis, which will be tested at the micro-level goes as follows.
- *Mobilization deficit hypothesis.* Political actors at the 2004 EP elections, namely parties and politicians, failed to make the relevance of the election clear to the voters and interest them in casting a ballot.
- *Political community deficit hypothesis.* Identification with Europe or the EU is too weak to generate political commitment and participation. More specifically, the basic claim is that European identity and the strength of political community are weaker in the East than in the West, contributing to the difference in turnout.
- *Political system deficit hypothesis.* This last hypothesis states that the outcome of the evaluation of particular features of the EU is too poor to generate commitment and participation.

The first hypothesis should explain aggregate turnout if turning out follows the same mechanisms as in the new member states of the EU. The following three sets of hypotheses aim at explaining individual turnout in a first step, and differences in turnout between countries in a second step.

The paper is organized as follows. In the next section a brief review will be presented of turnout in EP elections. Then the 'standard model' will be tested. Following this test, we undertake a theoretical exploration of the relationship between political community, evaluation, mobilization and turnout, and the presentation of the independent variables. After this, the individual-level turnout models will be evaluated and the resulting estimates compared to real turnout margins. The conclusion summarizes the results and evaluates its consequences.

Turnout at the European Parliament Elections 2004 Compared

The EP elections of 2004 mark a second historical juncture after the system transformations of 1989/1990 in Central and East Europe. Beside the fact that prior to these elections the EU experienced the biggest enlargement in its history, it was the first joint opportunity for the citizens to articulate their will and to determine who should become their representatives at the European level. In this sense, the 2004 elections were the 'Founding Elections' of a common Europe.

However, the election outcomes do not appear to reflect this historical significance. The elections mobilized a smaller proportion of voters than in any previous European Parliament elections. This continues a trend, which began as early as the second EP elections of 1984 and has continued unchanged. Electoral participation did not appear to indicate symbolic self-assignment to a political system at a level commensurate with the historical significance of the event. Thus, measured in terms of turnout, the EP elections of 2004 were nothing special: old patterns continued to hold true. From 1979 to 1999, on average, turnout dropped about 3.8 percentage points per election in the old member states, though not all countries experienced the same decline. Austria saw a decline of −12.6 since its first participation in 1996 and Finland the largest single decline of −28.9 percentage points between 1996 and 1999. In Great Britain turnout increased by 1.3 percentage points on average and, in Ireland, the highest single increase of 20.7 percentage points was seen, between 1984 and 1989. So the pattern saw considerable variation. However, on average, there was decline.

From 1999 to 2004, this decline is not dramatic with respect to the old member states (−0.2 percentage points). However, this is a continuation of the trend. More significant is the turnout in the new member states. Here, where it could have been a signal of self-assignment, many fewer voters felt attracted than in the old member states. Whereas in the old member states, on average, a little more than half of the electorate (52.7 per cent) went to the voting booth, in the new member countries only 40.3 per cent voted. And this figure is so high only because turnout in Malta and Cyprus was extraordinary high (71.2 and 82.4 per cent, respectively). The electorates of the new member states in Central and East Europe abstained by more than a two-thirds majority. Turnout there was, on average, as low as 31.2 per cent (Figure 1).

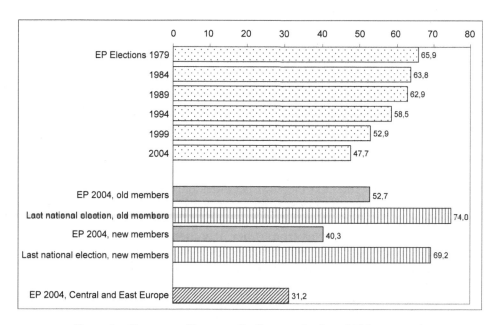

Figure 1.   Turnout at European Parliament elections 2004 compared.

The reason for low turnout at the European Parliament elections cannot be attributed to low turnout in Central and East Europe generally. Average turnout at the last national elections is somewhat lower than in the West, but not much. The so-called 'Euro-gap', the difference in turnout at national and the European elections, is considerable higher in the East.

The structural reasons for differences in turnout in general are well known: at the individual level these are age and social structure (Franklin 2002), at the country level compulsory voting and the position of EP elections in the national election cycle (Franklin, van der Eijck, and Oppenhuis 1996; Rose 2004; Schmitt 2005). These latter influences are the basis of the 'standard model' of EP election turnout to which we turn next.

Evaluating the 'Standard Model'

We address the question of whether the same forces operate in new as in established democracies by applying the 'standard model' of turnout at European Parliament elections established in past research (Franklin 2001, 2005). According to this model, turnout in these elections responds to just three independent variables: compulsory voting (countries that apply compulsion see much higher turnout), time until the next national election (as this time shrinks, turnout rises — except for compulsory voting countries) and whether the election is the first such election in the experience of the country concerned (countries, except for compulsory voting countries, see a 'first election boost' to their level of turnout). The model does not rule out the existence of other factors, which might share responsibility for turnout variations with the three variables mentioned, but no other variable suggested in past research proves significant when added to the standard model at the aggregate level. In particular, turnout at the most recent national election does not prove significant. Even though countries do vary in their levels of turnout at national elections, this variation (once we have controlled for compulsory voting) does not account for variations in turnout at EP elections.

Table 1 shows effects on turnout among established member countries in 2004 (Model Agg A, which is taken from Franklin 2005) and compares these effects with the effects on turnout when the dataset contains new member countries. When including new members it is necessary to decide how to treat the turnout gap between these and established members. If no allowance is made (as shown in Model Agg B), variance explained is considerably reduced, years until the next election becomes barely significant at the 0.05 level and the first election boost appears to vanish completely (the effect is smaller than its standard error). If we follow Rose's suggestion of distinguishing post-communist countries from other new members (as we do in Model Agg C), the model performs much better, though the effect of first election boost is substantially different from what it was in Model Agg A. If, instead of distinguishing post-communist new members from the rest, we instead distinguish just the five countries that had particularly low turnout in 2004, effects of other variables are essentially the same for new and established EU member states.

Table 1.   Comparing effects of the 'standard model' of turnout at European Parliament elections when new member countries are treated in different ways

Variable	Model Agg A[a] b	Model Agg B[b] b	Model Agg C[b] b	Model Agg D[b] b
(Constant)	52.9 (2.4)***	51.5 (3.0)***	52.5 (2.4)***	53.1 (2.4)***
Compulsory voting in country[c]	33.0 (3.0)***	33.6 (3.7)***	32.8 (2.9)***	32.2 (2.9)***
Years until next national election[d]	−2.8 (0.8)***	−2.2 (1.1)*	−2.6 (0.8)**	−2.8 (0.8)***
First EP election held in country[d]	10.9 (2.9)***	1.5 (3.1)	13.3 (2.9)***	9.9 (2.7)***
Post-communist country			−29.7 (4.1)***	
Low-turnout country				−34.0 (4.6)***
Adjusted variance explained	0.806	0.684	0.803	0.805
n	79	89	89	89

[a]From Franklin (2005) — aggregate data from 1979 to 2004 omitting countries that were new members in 2004.
[b]Aggregate data from 1979 to 2004, all available cases.
[c]Treating Italy as 0.875, 0.75, 0.675 of a compulsory voting country in 1994, 1999 and 2004 (see text).
[d]Except for compulsory voting countries (coded 0).
***significant at 0.001; **significant at 0.01; *significant at 0.05.

This model tells us that new member countries can be seen to have behaved just like established member countries in 2004, so long as we model the particularly low turnout registered by five of them. In all countries (including the five with particularly low turnout) it is reasonable to assume that a first election boost was in fact experienced,[1] in all countries there is an apparently identical effect of time until the next election, and in all countries the effect of compulsory voting (or the lack of it) appears very similar.[2]

These findings are quite encouraging. It does not appear that citizens of the new member states are reacting differently to European Parliament elections than citizens of established member states.[3] Our task is now to establish, if we can, why these five countries displayed such very low turnout. Note that it is still an open question whether the five states with particularly low turnout should be distinguished from other post-communist states. If we cannot find anything that distinguishes them from the other post-communist states (but can find something that distinguishes all post-communist states from other member states), this would not do violence to our aggregate-level findings. Though Model Agg D does appear to perform better than Model Agg C, the differences are certainly not statistically significant.

Political Evaluations, Political Community, Mobilization and Turnout

Franklin (2001, 2004, 2005) has pointed out several times that the real puzzle regarding European Parliament elections is not that turnout in these elections is so low but rather that turnout in these elections is as high as observed empirically. Objectively speaking, these elections provide no means by which voters could observe a linkage between their votes and the policy outputs of the European Union. To the extent that voters perceive this lack of linkage, this would provide an excellent explanation for their failure to vote; and, to the extent that the realization dawns on voters that EP elections have no purpose, we can expect turnout at these elections to fall still further. The EP elections of 2004 provide an excellent opportunity for us to investigate the distribution of relevant evaluations to see whether they correspond to differences in EP election turnout.

We are encouraged in this search by a particular feature of post-communist member states that might make citizens of these democracies particularly responsive to differentiation along the suggested lines. In established democracies, habits of voting deriving from experience at national elections are entrenched (Franklin 2004). It seems clear that these entrenched habits among established voters maintain a higher level of turnout at EP elections than we would otherwise see. Electorates of post-communist countries, by contrast, have not necessarily had time for such habits to become entrenched. So evaluations of the utility of voting should play a larger part in determining overall turnout in post-communist countries, easily explaining the very low turnout among some of these.

Perceptions of linkage between votes and policy consequences require a reciprocal relationship between electors and elected. On the one hand, there is a simple instrumental consideration: elections ought to translate distributions of preferences of the electorate into a distribution of preferences of representatives in parliament. Thus, elections should provide an effective translation of preferences and guarantee the responsiveness of the political institutions and actors. If this is a correct perception of what voters expect, then elections will be meaningful only as and in so far as they provide these outputs. If they do, it is worthwhile for individuals to vote — if not, not.

This consideration is directly related to the *political system deficit hypothesis*. If the system leaves the voters with the impression that elections neither provide an effective translation of preferences nor guarantee responsiveness by those elected, the system has a deficit and voters have less reason to vote.

However, there is more to elections than the output side of the system. The other side of the coin is the participation of citizens in elections. Democracy is more than an instrumental mechanism linking rulers and ruled. The acceptance of the rules of the game (procedures as well as decisions) call for support by affective generalization, which is self-assigned, and identification with the political order (Fuchs 1999; Fuchs and Klingemann 2002). If this is true, identification with the political community should matter for turnout. The relationship of elections to political community can be demonstrated by looking to the functions of elections. Rose and Mossawir (1969) define the function of elections as follows: elections allow citizens (1) to select representatives, (2) to exchange influence, (3) to develop an identification with the system, (4) to satisfy expressive needs and (5) to express distance from the system. Or elections can be meaningless, because they do not allow (6) choices, or do not generate affiliation and identification with the system. Part of these functions relates to the instrumental, part to the affective aspects of democracy and democratic elections. Instrumental or output-related aspects are particularly relevant to points 1 and 2. 'The emphasis here is upon the extent to which the need for election or re-election will lead incumbents and candidates to alter their policies in order to retain or gain office' (Rose and Mossawir 1969, 170). Elections should, however, not only be effective, but should also produce an affection of citizens for the norms and symbols of the system (points 2 and 3). They should 'contribute to the development or maintenance of an individual's allegiance to the existing constitutional regime' (*ibid.*, 171). These functions lead in a general sense to a commitment and identification with the political community. Mackenzie has described the route to identification in the following way: 'It may be said that electoral procedure is functionally analogous to procedure in a marriage ceremony: "Do you take this man (or women) to be your lawfully wedded husband (or wife)?" "I do". The point in time at which "I do" is said is not psychologically a moment of choice or decision — that came earlier; it is the point at which an individual preference becomes a social commitment' (Mackenzie and Rokkan 1968, 5).

This argument relates directly to turnout and its relationship to political community and thus to the *political community deficit hypothesis*. If it is true that the decision to participate electorally is prior to the choice made between parties, and the reason for this is the social commitment to the political order, feeling part of a European political community should matter for turnout.

However, given the fact that elections should generate a reciprocal relationship between electors and elected, it can also be claimed that not only voters have a duty to deliver to the system, but also political actors and representatives. As already mentioned, they should be responsive. But in a democracy with competitive elections this is not all. They also have to get their messages to the people. This message is two-fold from their perspective. Clearly it is in their own interest to demonstrate the difference of their political offerings from the ones of their competitors, and thus to make choices meaningful. Beside this, it is also in their interests to (re-)produce the attachment of the people to the system by mobilization. This is more or less in line with the huge debate about a European public. The foreign minister of the Federal Republic of Germany claims in a paper: 'Generating a public means to generate the cement for the future of any political order. Without a minimum of political public, the European Union cannot develop further'. A public does not come into being automatically. A public is a forum that needs speakers, mediators, and an audience (Neidhardt, Koopmans, and Pfetsch 2000). Election campaigns are the ideal occasion to generate a public — at least temporarily. It seems natural to assume that the speakers at these times are candidates, parties and other officials.

However, if such actors do not care, why should voters? Given the observation, that turnout in EP elections is rather low than high, the *mobilization deficit hypothesis* comes into play: the less the efforts made to inform and mobilize the electorates, the less the turnout.

If the claim of the three hypotheses is correct, turnout should be influenced (1) instrumentally, by the degree to which elections are seen to be effective and the system to be responsive, (2) by the degree of identification with the political community, and (3) by efforts of political actors to inform and mobilize the public.

In this paper, we employ a set of indicators that are well suited to test our hypotheses. One battery of questions covers the attitudinal, instrumental and affective aspects — namely matters of electoral effectiveness, political responsiveness and European political community. The following seven questions were asked:

For each of the following propositions, please tell me if it rather corresponds or rather does not correspond to your attitude or your opinion:

a. It is very important for you which particular political party gained the most seats in the European Parliament elections
b. It is very important for you which particular candidates win seats and become MEPs in the European Parliament elections
c. The European Parliament takes into consideration the concerns of European citizens
d. You trust the institutions of the European Union
e. The membership of [COUNTRY] in the European Union is a good thing
f. You feel you are a citizen of the European Union
g. You feel attached to Europe

Possible answers: 'Yes, rather'; 'No, rather not'; 'Don't know/no answer'.
EOS Gallup (2004).

Items (a) and (b) are directly related to electoral effectiveness. They contain the evaluation of whether it makes a difference who gets the majority and, thus, whom to vote for. If voters assume that it is important who gets seats and which party gains most seats, this implies that they assume that voting makes a difference.

Responsiveness characterizes the ability of political actors, political institutions and the system as a whole to react to needs and demands of the citizens. Item (c) is an evaluation of the European Parliament in this regard. An indirect indicator of the perception of responsiveness might be the trust in the EU (item (d)). Trust is an investment in the future based on the assumption that the one who is trusted will behave according to one's expectations. Trust will be provided if the experience is that actors have behaved in the past according to expectations and will do so in the future. Thus, trust can be read as an indicator of responsiveness.

Finally, items (e), (f) and (g) relate to identification with the political community. Item (e) is somewhat more evaluative than the clearly affective items (f) and (g). But it also relates to the affective or generalized aspect of the country's belonging to the community.

Although, the items can be sorted clearly in analytical terms, the open question is whether voters do the same. In order to explore the dimensionality of the item battery, an exploratory factor analysis was performed. The result is clearly in line with expectations. Three factors could be extracted, with loadings separating clearly between effectiveness, responsiveness and community (Table 2).

A second battery of questions relates to central aspects of mobilization in election campaigns. Election campaigns are generally the periods in which attention of the citizens to the political system is increased and attachment actualized. The cyclical development of political interest, party support and attentiveness between elections supports this observation. Furthermore, it has been shown that support for European integration also follows this path. European election campaigns serve to re-actualize and re-mobilize support (Weßels 1995).

The expectation from this is very clear: election campaigns should also generate electoral participation. What are traditionally the channels of information and mobilization that can be assumed? The most central role in political communication is played by the mass media. Secondly, information-seeking also plays an important role. Thirdly, in election campaigns, the more or less direct communication between voters and candidates or

Table 2. Dimensions of attitudes towards Europe: political community, effectiveness, and responsiveness, 2004

Indicator	Political community	Effectiveness	Responsiveness
You feel attached to Europe	**0.854**	0.093	0.087
You feel you are a citizen of the European Union	**0.795**	0.089	0.236
The membership of [COUNTRY] in the European Union is a good thing	**0.514**	0.085	0.503
It is very important for you which particular political party gained the most seats in the European Parliament elections	0.091	**0.864**	0.055
It is very important for you which particular candidates win seats and become MEPs in the European Parliament elections	0.074	**0.855**	0.115
You trust the institutions of the European Union	0.088	0.075	**0.847**
The European Parliament takes into consideration the concerns of European citizens	0.267	0.131	**0.753**
Proportion of 'explained' variance	0.389	0.184	0.122

Pooled data, twenty-five countries; 24,063 respondents; samples of almost equal size.
Possible answers: Yes, No, Don't know, No Answer. Coding: 1 (Yes), 0 (Don't know, No Answer) and —1 (No).
Bold: Variable loads strongest on the respective dimension.
Source: EOS Gallup (2004).

parties normally reaches its heights. It is likely that these three means of political information serve different purposes: the media producing the agenda, information-seeking producing choices, and direct contacts producing mobilization. However, it is beyond the scope of this paper to explore this. Rather, the information and mobilization environment of electorates will be explored, and related to turnout. The questions we used read as follows:

Political parties and candidates campaigned for votes in the European Parliament elections we have just had. For each of the following, please tell me if you have been in this situation or not ...

a. You have seen or heard things concerning the electoral campaign on television or on the radio
b. You have seen advertisements for parties or candidates
c. You have read about the electoral campaign in the newspapers
d. You received leaflets concerning the European Elections in your mail-box
e. You have been contacted by political parties or candidates or their representatives by phone
f. Political parties or candidates or their representatives called to your home
g. You have been approached in the street by political parties or candidates or their representatives
h. You have searched for information on the European Elections on the internet
i. You took part in public gatherings or meetings concerning the European Parliament Elections
j. You have discussed the European Parliament Elections with your family, friends or acquaintances
k. You have been aware of a non-party campaign or advertisement encouraging people to vote in the European Parliament elections

Possible answers: Yes, No, Don't know, No Answer.
EOS Gallup (2004).

The items cover the three relevant aspects of information and mobilization. Items (a)–(d) deal with mediated information; information-seeking is covered by items (h)–(k); items (e)–(g) refer to direct contacts of candidates and parties with voters.

Again, a factor analysis was performed to check the dimensionality of these items and to reduce their complexity. The result fits the distinction between mediated information, information-seeking and direct contacting very nicely. Media or mediated information items account for most of the variance, followed by direct contacts. Information-seeking is the 'weakest' factor, but still accounts for 10 per cent of the inter-item variation (Table 3).

Table 3.   Dimensions of mobilization in the European elections 2004 — information channels

Items	Factor 1 Media	Factor 2 Contacts	Factor 3 Info-seeking
You have seen or heard things concerning the electoral campaign on television or on the radio	**0.6608**	−0.0513	−0.0223
You have seen advertisements for parties or candidates	**0.6537**	0.0506	0.0032
You have read about the electoral campaign in the newspapers	**0.6275**	−0.0100	0.2575
You received leaflets concerning the European Elections in your mailbox	**0.4728**	0.3281	−0.1919
Political parties or candidates or their representatives called to your home	−0.0517	**0.6670**	0.0508
You have been contacted by political parties or candidates or their representatives by phone	0.0714	**0.7192**	−0.0599
You have been approached in the street by political parties or candidates or their representatives	0.0612	**0.5368**	0.2275
You have searched for information on the European Elections on the internet	−0.0223	−0.0266	**0.7414**
You took part in public gatherings or meetings concerning the European Parliament Elections	−0.0274	0.3238	**0.5263**
You have discussed the European Parliament Elections with your family, friends or acquaintances	0.4321	−0.0091	**0.4415**
You have been aware of a non-party campaign or advertisement encouraging people to vote in the European Parliament elections	0.3152	0.0410	**0.3254**
'Explained' variance (in %)	18.8	12.5	9.9

Pooled analysis, twenty-five countries.
Possible answers: Yes, No, Don't know, No Answer. Coding: 1 (Yes), 0 (No, Don't know, No Answer).
Bold: Variable loads strongest on the respective dimension.
Source: EOS Gallup (2004).

For a first exploration of the relationship between political evaluations and European identity on the one hand, and political information and mobilization on the other hand, factor scales were recoded and related to means of reported turnout.

Results can be reported straightforwardly. According to the *system deficit hypothesis*, turnout should be the lower the less effective the elections and the less responsive the system. As can be seen in Table 4, this is indeed the case. Individuals who show a factor score value smaller than half a standard deviation below the mean report, on average, a turnout of 39.5 and 50.0 per cent, respectively. For those, showing scale values higher than a half standard deviation above the mean, turnout is 77.3 and 69.2 per cent, respectively. In terms of correlation (Eta), effectiveness has the clearer impact than responsiveness. The *political community deficit hypothesis* claims that low identity goes with low turnout, strong identity with high turnout. Again, this pattern can be observed across all individuals in the

Table 4.   Turnout in per cent, depending on attitudinal evaluations, and levels of information and mobilization, 2004

	Low	Medium	High	Eta
Attitudinal evaluations				
Community	51.0	64.8	64.1	0.126
Responsiveness	50.0	61.6	69.2	0.168
Effectiveness	39.5	68.0	77.3	0.347
Information and mobilization				
Media	48.6	60.3	68.8	0.156
Contacts	56.2	58.5	72.9	0.120
Info-seeking	52.1	60.5	72.4	0.139

Low: Factor scale value < −0.5 standard deviation.
Medium: −0.5 to +0.5 standard deviation.
High: >+0.5 standard deviation.
$n = 24,063$.
Source: EOS Gallup (2004).

analysis. The pooled analysis shows that these differences are true despite country-level differences.

Table 4 additionally reports results in a similar fashion for the three factors of information and mobilization. The *mobilization deficit hypothesis* claims that the lower the information/mobilization level, the lower the turnout. This is indeed the case. The difference in turnout between the lowest and the highest levels of mediated information, information-seeking, and direct contacts is roughly around twenty percentage points. Correlations (Eta) of all three factors are rather similar.

These descriptive results all speak in favour of the hypotheses. Do these findings hold up in a multivariate analysis? The simple answer is 'yes'.

Model IndA in Table 5 tests just the impact of the standard socio-economic and demographic indicators on voting participation. These variables serve as controls for the two alternative models. This model produces the expected outcome. The older, the better educated, the higher in professional status and the more urban their residences, the more likely individuals are to turn out. However, rural area is not significant and the explained variance is low, as could have been expected (Table 5, first column).

By adding the six independent variables which encompass the attitudinal and information/mobilization hypotheses, the result of model IndB shows an increase of explained variance to 16 per cent in reported turnout. All effects except rural area are significant (Table 5, second column). Among the attitudinal variables, electoral effectiveness has the largest effect. This indicates that if people are of the opinion that that their votes have no effect, they regard it as useless to vote. Other aspects being constant, the probability of participation in the European elections of 2004 increases by 52 per cent if effectiveness increases by one scale point. All other individual-level variables increase the probability by somewhat more than 20 per cent, except for party

Table 5. Regressing individual turnout in European Parliament elections 2004 on demographic and social characteristics, political attitudes, mobilization factors and macro-characteristics

	Model IndA	Model IndB	Model IndC
Age in years	0.056	0.056	0.056
Age in years, squared	0.000	0.000	0.000
Education, age when finished	0.083	0.083	0.083
Worker	−0.220	−0.328	−0.220
Rural area	−0.009 n.s.	0.013 n.s.	−0.009 n.s.
Political community		0.214	0.204
Effectiveness		0.519	0.489
Responsiveness		0.260	0.225
Media		0.251	0.328
Contacts		0.264	0.233
Information-seeking		0.257	0.294
Party identification		0.431	0.377
Compulsory voting			1.705
Years left to next national elections			0.184
Constant	−2.322	−1.606	−2.322
Pseudo-R^2	0.037	0.156	0.199
n	23,725	23,725	23,725

Three models (logistic regression, robust standard errors).
Education: 0 never full-time to school; 1 up to 15; 2 up to 21; 3 to 21 and older.
Party identification: 1 feeling close or very close to one of the political parties; 0 not feeling close, don't know/no answer.
Source: EOS Gallup (2004).

identification, which contributes 40 per cent to the probability of turning out. As observed by Franklin (2004, 164), party identification serves to keep turnout high when other factors that might have generated high turnout are absent. It is related to the 'entrenched habits' of voting mentioned earlier — the absence of which in post-communist societies should make these countries especially vulnerable to lesser instrumental, affective and mobilizational reasons for voting.

Adding the two most important macro-variables of the 'standard model' — compulsory voting and years left to the next national elections — increases explained variance to 20 per cent, while hardly affecting the influence of individual-level variables. The most influential factor is, of course, compulsory voting. However, the position of EP elections in the national elections cycle has a strong effect, also.

The question remains whether the introduction of micro-level variables can account for the effect of the low-turnout countries variable introduced in model Agg D of the 'standard model' earlier. The proof of the pudding lies in whether individual-level models correctly estimate real election outcomes in terms of turnout. In a first step, the estimate of model IndB, which contains only individual-level variables, is tested. Comparing the mean of the estimated individual probabilities results in a somewhat poorer replication of real turnout figures than the aggregate 'standard model' Agg B (explained variance of real turnout by estimated turnout 54 per cent). Furthermore, the probability estimates of model IndB clearly are too high, compared to real turnout. The regression coefficient indicates that, at the lower end, probabilities overestimate turnout by a ratio about 3: 1. At the higher end, there is no overestimation (not shown).

Adding to this model the two central macro-variables of the aggregate 'standard model' clearly improves the turnout estimates. The mean of the individual-level estimates of the probability to vote reproduces 75 per cent of the variance of the real turnout figures (Figure 2). Compared to the aggregate 'standard model' Agg B, this is a significantly higher proportion. It comes close to the 80 per cent explained by adding to this model the unexplicated dummy variable for low-turnout countries (model Agg D). However, although the relative position of the countries with regard to official turnout can be reproduced quite well, this model still provides estimates, which are 5–7 per cent higher than real turnout in the low-turnout area.

Again, this overestimation does not exist for high levels of turnout, but, in any case, the divergence is no greater than the overestimate of turnout in

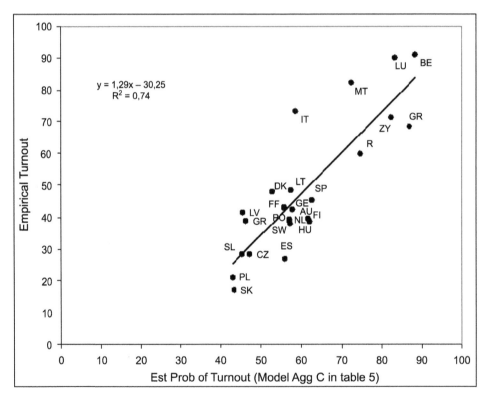

Figure 2.   Aggregate estimation: turnout and turnout estimated by levels of European attitudes, mobilization and compulsory voting compared.

Greece, for example, or the underestimate in Italy or Malta. Effectively, the model does an outstanding job of predicting turnout in all sorts of democracies, established as well as post-communist.

Conclusion: Do Mobilization and Attitudes Equal Turnout?

The 2004 elections mark a historical juncture, because they can be regarded as the 'Founding Elections' of a common Europe of East and West, which has overcome the obsolete 'Iron Curtain'. However, the electorates obviously did not feel that way. This paper began by pointing out that the idea of explaining low turnout as a consequence of post-communism in new member countries cannot be true. The aggregate 'standard model' of EP turnout introduced by Franklin (2001, 2005), however, can cope with the 2004 European elections only if low-turnout country is introduced as a variable. The main purpose of this paper has been to account for the lower turnout in some countries, by finding variables that capture theoretically based reasons for these differences. We introduced individual-level attitudinal concepts related to political community and evaluations of the EU political system, and a mobilization concept. For the attitudinal concepts, we put forward three deficit hypotheses, deriving from the expectation that each of the related factors contributes positively or negatively to turnout. That the hypotheses are formulated in terms of deficits is because of the fact that turnout in the 2004 European elections was so unexpectedly low.

Thus, the basic assumption tested in this paper is that there are deficits — deficits in the strength of the political community, deficits in the institutional system of the EU and deficits in mobilization of individuals to vote. Introducing these factors into a model of individual turnout shows that there is indeed quite an impact on turnout. The effect is strongest for the perceived effectiveness of electoral institutions of the EU. Slightly smaller effects are shown by political community, responsiveness of the EU and the mobilization factors (media, contacts and information-seeking) which, however, show a very similar degree of impact on individual turnout. The attitudinal and mobilization variables alone, however, do not contribute much to the explanation of real turnout in the twenty-five EU countries. Adding the two central variables from the aggregate 'standard model' of turnout (i.e. compulsory voting and the position of the EP elections in the national election cycle) results in a model that can explain differences in country-level turnout to quite an impressive extent. Thus, the results clearly point to the fact that factors closely related to the EU and to mobilization efforts in EP elections contribute to differences in turnout. Thus, post-communism, the factor Richard Rose regards as responsible, is not a factor needed to explain low turnout in certain countries. Indeed, our theoretically based variables explain turnout variations not only as between post-communist and established EU member countries but also within members of each of these groups of countries.

It is certainly not false to conclude from these results that political actors, namely candidates, parties and EU officials have to put more effort into making clear to the voter that voting makes a difference, and to inform and mobilize them. Although the traditional model of democracy is very much a bottom-up model, this is not true in reality. As much as citizens should feel the commitment to the political order and the duty to engage, political actors should feel the duty to attract and to attach citizens to that order. Obviously, there is a way to do this — otherwise we would not have found such clear country differences.

Still, a graver problem than simply a mobilization deficit afflicts European Parliament elections — a problem that may be responsible for low mobilization effects as well as having more direct effects on turnout. This is the strong belief held by European citizens that European Parliament elections serve no purpose. The impact shown in Table 5 of people's perception that the outcome of EP elections does not matter is stronger than the impact of any other variable apart from compulsory voting; the bivariate correlation of this variable with turnout is shown to be twice that of any other individual-level variable (Table 4). If potential voters feel this way about European Parliament elections, it can be assumed that mobilizing agencies (parties, interest groups and the media) feel much the same. So it may be quixotic of us to call for greater efforts to get out the vote for elections that manifestly serve little purpose. It would certainly be more pertinent to provide a meaningful rationale for EP elections so that not only voters see a reason for voting but also mobilizing agencies see the point in expending resources on getting out the vote.

Notes

1. The extent of the first election boost among low-turnout countries cannot be estimated separately, since its magnitude simply alters the estimated turnout gap between these countries and the rest. However, the other five new member states show virtually the same pattern as established member states in this regard.
2. Again, it is not possible to tell whether the effect is the same for the five low-turnout countries, since any deviation for these countries from the general pattern will be taken up by the dummy variable distinguishing them from other countries. Italy abolished compulsory voting in 1993. On the basis of logic developed in Franklin (2004), we expect this abolition to have a progressive effect on turnout as the electorate progressively loses more and more of those who learned the habit of voting while a compulsion was in effect. Hence the proportions applied to compulsory voting in Italy at successive EP elections (Franklin 2005).
3. This conclusion can only be tentative for the five states with particularly low turnout — see notes 1 and 2 above.

References

EOS Gallup. 2004. *Europe Flash EB 162 'Post European Elections 2004 Survey'* (21/06/2004–30/06/2004). Brussels: EP (DG Information) and the EC (DG Press).

Franklin, M.N. 2001. How structural factors cause turnout variations at European Parliament elections. *European Union Politics* 2, no. 3: 309–28.

Franklin, M.N. 2002. The dynamic of electoral participation. In *Comparing democracies 2. New challenges in the study of elections and voting*, eds. L. LeDuc, R.G. Niemi and P. Norris, 148–68. London: Sage.

Franklin, M.N. 2004. *Voter turnout and the dynamics of electoral competition in established democracies since 1945*. New York: Cambridge University Press.

Franklin, M.N. 2005. European elections and the European voter. In *European Union: Power and policy-making*. 3rd edn, ed. J. Richardson, 201–15. London: Longman.

Franklin, M.N., C. van der Eijck, and E. Oppenhuis. 1996. The institutional context: Turnout. In *Choosing Europe*, eds. C. van der Eijck and M.N. Franklin, 306–31. Ann Arbor: Univ. of Michigan Press.

Fuchs, D. 1999. The democratic culture of unified Germany. In *Critical citizens: Global support for democratic government*, ed. P. Norris, 123–45. Oxford: Oxford Univ. Press.

Fuchs, D., and H.-D. Klingemann. 2002. Eastward enlargement of the European Union and the identity of Europe. *West European Politics* 25, no. 2: 19–54.

Mackenzie, W.J.M., and S. Rokkan. 1968. Elections. In *International encyclopedia of the social sciences*, ed. D.L. Sills, 1–21. New York: Macmillan.

Neidhardt, F., R. Koopmans, and B. Pfetsch. 2000. Konstitutionsbedingungen politischer Öffentlichkeit: Der Fall Europa. In *Zur Zukunft der Demokratie*, eds. H.-D. Klingemann and F. Neidhardt, 263–94. Berlin: edition sigma.

Rose, R. 2004. *Europe expands, turnout falls: The significance of the 2004 European Parliament election*. Stockholm: International Institute for Democracy and Electoral Assistance.

Rose, R., and H. Mossawir. 1969. Voting and elections. A functional analysis. In *Empirical democratic theory*, eds. C. Cnudde and D.E. Neubauer, 69–97. Chicago: Markham.

Schmitt, H. 2005. The European Parliament elections of June 2004. Still second-order?. Mannheim: unpublished manuscript.

Weßels, B. 1995. Evaluations of the EC: Elite or mass-driven?. In *Public opinion and internationalized governance*, eds. O. Niedermayer and R. Sinnott, 137–62. Oxford: Oxford Univ. Press.

Vote Switching in European Parliament Elections: Evidence from June 2004

MICHAEL MARSH

Trinity College, University of Dublin, Dublin, Ireland

ABSTRACT   This article assesses a number of explanations for vote switching in European Parliament elections. These include the theories of surge and decline and referendum voting, advanced to explain mid-term elections in the US as well as the theory of EP elections as second order national elections. Hypotheses deriving from each theory are set out and a number of tests conducted with data from the 2004 European election study. It concludes that each theory offers something of value without any theory being obviously dominant. We also see some significant differences in patterns of vote switching in new and old member states.

Introduction

The fifth set of elections to the European Parliament in 2004 saw twenty-five countries sending representatives to the parliament in Brussels and Strasbourg, more than twice the number who participated in the first elections in 1979. On the face of it this presents anyone wishing to understand what happens at these elections with a great deal more variety and uncertainty than previously, but this would ignore the fact that we have learned a lot about European Parliament elections in the last twenty-five years. We have observed significant regularities in the behaviour of European voters and have developed a theory — second-order election theory — which provides a sensible account of such regularities. On this basis we certainly have a set

Correspondence Address: Michael Marsh, Trinity College, University of Dublin, Dublin 2, Ireland. E-mail: mmarsh@tcd.ie of expectations about what will happen not just in the fifteen countries who participated in the last election of 1999 but also in those who participated for the first time in 2004.

This is not to say that our expectations are very precise, nor that our theory is without blemish. Uncertainty remains to cloud any predictions, and there remain both features of behaviour that are unexplained by theory, as well as facts that fit uncomfortably with it. This paper reviews the performance of the theory of second-order elections to date, and also considers the alternative merits of two theories developed to explain regularities in the behaviour of US voters in the congressional elections that occur in presidential mid-term, which show significant parallels with those of European Parliament elections. Elections to parliaments within member states are held according to various timetables. Occasionally national and EP elections coincide (they always do in Luxembourg); more typically they do not, but fall somewhere within the national parliamentary election cycle in each member state. While those elected to the European Parliament sit in European Party Groups, they are elected on national party lists and, hence, it is possible to compare the performance of national parties in European Parliament elections with their performance in the preceding national election. It is also possible to compare turnout. When we do so we observe two fairly general patterns: governments lose votes compared to the preceding national election and turnout falls. In the USA there are national elections every two years for Congress and every four years for the President. Congressional elections take place coincidentally with presidential elections and again in the middle of a president's term of office — a 'mid-term' election. Congressional mid-term elections differ from the preceding congressional election in two respects: the president's party wins fewer votes and turnout is lower. This pattern has endured throughout the twentieth century, almost without exception.

The theories discussed here have generally sought to link the regularities in each context, to see the turnout and government or presidential loss as connected rather than separate phenomena. In the European context it is a central aspect of the theory of 'second order national elections' (Reif and Schmitt 1980; Reif 1985, 1997). In the US context this is the contribution made by the theory of 'surge and decline' advanced by Angus Campbell (1960, 1966). A further common aspect of each theoretical approach is that the results of the less important election are seen as interpretable only through an understanding of something exogenous. In the European case this is the national parliamentary election cycle; in the US case this is the presidential election cycle.

In the next section we will review two sets of theory. Special attention will be given to two things. First, what is the source of the explanation and, secondly, what is the mechanism of decision making at the level of the individual that provides the expected change. Having done that we can then move on to consider the manner in which these theories can be applied to the 2004 European Parliament elections, what they explain and what they do not explain.

Second-Order Theory and Some Alternatives

Second-Order Theory

The concept of a second-order national election in fact has its roots in observations of electoral patterns in US mid-term elections, as well as German regional elections, but it was used by Reif and Schmitt (1980) as an explanation of the results of the first direct European Parliament election. Reif and Schmitt point out that elections differ in terms of how important people think they are and assume national general elections will be considered more important than European Parliament elections. Rather than distinguish elections as such they refer to different arenas of politics, with elections to bodies in the most important arena of primary importance and elections in other arenas of lesser consequence.[1] As long as national politics remain pre-eminent, general elections in parliamentary democracies are first-order elections. All others are second-order. Voters can be expected to behave differently in the two types of elections because of their differential importance. For a start, they will be less likely to vote in second-order elections because they and the parties know that such elections are less important. When they do turn out, voters will be more mindful of the political situation in the first-order arena than that of the second-order arena. First-order issues, for instance, will dominate second-order ones.[2] In particular, voters may take the opportunity to signal their dissatisfaction with government policy despite the fact that the second-order election has no direct implications for government composition. Additionally, in making their choice, voters are more inclined to follow their 'heart' in second-order elections, whose relative un-importance means there are no consequences. This explains why their behaviour may differ from that in first-order elections, in which voters tend to follow their 'head'.

Although Reif and Schmitt do not develop a proper theory of the voter, some points are implicit in what they say. Essentially, at the core of second-order theory is a relatively strategic voter who has a preference structure across two or more parties with more than one non-zero element. In other words, a voter does not simply support one party and reject the rest.

This strategic aspect can be developed further. Reif and Schmitt suggested that governments would perform particularly poorly when second-order elections occurred at mid-term. The rationale for this is that mid-term is a normal nadir of government popularity, brought about by a combination of popularity cycles, and the inevitability of unrealized expectations (see below). However, this is disputed by Oppenhuis, van der Eijk, and Franklin (1996), who question the existence of such popularity cycles and instead focus on the importance of the election as a signalling device. This is also a function of the time since the last general election, and the time expected until the next one. When a second-order election follows closely, or is simultaneous with, a general election, it passes almost unnoticed. Hence, turnout will be particularly low (but not in the case of concurrent elections where turnout in both contests tends to be at the same level). Those who do vote will please themselves, voting with the 'heart'. However, when a second-order election takes place on the eve of a general election, its importance as a sign of what will happen at that general election is considerable. In such circumstances turnout will be rather high (relative to other second-order elections) and voters are more likely to signal their discontent with a party or government. The 'referendum' element of second-order elections is thus contextually located, not by levels of government dissatisfaction or economic trends but by the timing of the second-order election in the first-order election cycle.

A second development of second-order theory is the suggestion that the differential importance of elections is better represented by a continuum than by a categorization (Van der Eijk and Franklin et al. 1996). Not all second-order elections are equally unimportant but not all first-order elections are equally important either. In fact, where general elections have few implications for the choice of government, because a system of consociational democracy operates for instance, then they may differ little from second-order elections in the same system. Perhaps only in countries where general elections are expected to bring about some alternation of government control does it make sense to see local or European parliament elections as second-order.

We now turn to some alternative theoretical approaches, developed to account for US mid-term election results. We begin with the theory of surge and decline, and then deal more fully with the so-called referendum element of such elections, already alluded to above.

Surge and Decline

The original theory of surge and decline was presented by Angus Campbell (1960). We call this 'Campbell_1'. The theory seeks to explain differences in turnout and support for the president's party between mid-term and preceding presidential elections in the USA, but Campbell himself saw it as having a more general relevance. In his original formulation of surge and decline theory, Campbell (1960, 62) suggested that although the theory was specifically intended to illuminate well-established patterns in US political behaviour it was likely that 'the basic concepts ... — political stimulation, political interest, party identification, core voters and peripheral voters, and high- and low-stimulus elections — are equally applicable to an understanding of political behaviour in other democratic system'.

The expectation is that in presidential elections people are likely to depart from their 'normal' pattern of political behaviour. This is because such elections are (relatively, in the US context) high stimulus elections. The higher stimulus of a presidential election promotes two types of change. First, it draws those to the polls who do not usually vote, those Campbell calls 'peripheral' voters. Lacking a strong party attachment, peripheral voters are likely to be swayed disproportionately by the circumstances of the moment to vote for the winning party. At the next mid-term election, these voters stay at home, thus adversely affecting the president's party. The high stimulus also means that regular, or 'core' voters are more likely to be swayed by the advantage circumstances give to the winning party to depart from their normal partisan behaviour, only to return to their habitual behaviour in the lower-stimulus mid-term. Again, this is to the disadvantage of the president's party. Presidential elections are thus a departure from an equilibrium that is restored at the subsequent congressional election.

After reviewing some individual-level evidence and arguing that it does not support classic surge and decline theory, James Campbell (1993) provides a revised version of surge and decline in which the mechanism of a higher/ lower stimulus remains much the same but the impact of that on different types of voters changes. We call this 'Campbell_2'. On the basis that the individual-level evidence does not support the differential turnout of independent voters in the two types of election, James Campbell argues instead that the difference in the result is caused by the return to the mid-term electorate of partisans of the losing party in the previous election ('disadvantaged partisans') who were cross-pressured by short-term forces and abstained, and the switching back of weaker partisans who defected due to the same cross-pressures. In his revised version of surge and decline theory it is strong partisans who move from abstention to voting, and weak partisans and independents who switch. The important concept in the revised model is that of cross-pressure. Strong partisans may find themselves cross-pressured in a presidential year, wanting to vote for their normal party but preferring the candidate of the opposition. They resolve the conflict by abstaining. Weaker partisans have no problem with the cross-pressures and simply switch parties. 'Campbell_2' is a revision of 'Campbell_1'.

Referendum Theory

A quite different explanation for mid-term losses is the referendum theory advanced by Tufte (1975). In sharp contrast to surge and decline, which finds the roots of inter-election decline in the upsurge at the previous election, referendum theory locates it in the record of the administration. However, as in surge and decline theory, the roots remain external to the election itself, since they are located in the record of the administration rather than of Congress. Mid-term elections are essentially a referendum on the government's performance, in which voters express their approval or disapproval through voting for or against those representing the president's party. The mechanism of change lies in the decision by at least some mid-term voters to reward or punish the party of the president. The election provides an occasion at which voters can signal their dissatisfaction. This view is expressed most clearly by Tufte and we refer to his theory as 'referendum'.

Tufte considers two separate causes of approval: the public's general satisfaction with the president's performance and the trends in economic development. His analysis uses these to predict the magnitude of swings against the incumbent party, and he shows these can be predicted with a high degree of accuracy. There is nothing in the theory of a referendum itself to explain why swings are almost always adverse, but Tufte suggests that this stems from two further trends. The first is that presidential popularity tends to decline through a term of office; the second is that the performance of the economy tends to be better at the time of presidential elections. Of course, to the extent that neither is the case, the president's party should not suffer at mid-term.

Unlike surge and decline, Tufte's referendum theory does not directly link turnout and mid-term loss but others have attempted to do so within referendum theory. Kernell (1977) asserts a 'negativity' hypothesis. Like Tufte, Kernell sees the mid-term election as strongly influenced by perceptions of the president's record but he offers a more fundamental account of why this is bad news for the president's party. According to Kernell, judgements on presidential performance are always biased in a negative direction because — as a social-psychological rule — negative impressions are always more salient than positive ones. Moreover, voters are more likely to act on negative impressions. Hence, there will be more people dissatisfied with the president than there were two years ago; dissatisfied voters will also be more likely to turn out than satisfied ones and, having turned out, will be more likely to vote against the president's party.[3]

Having outlined various theories we now turn to examine their relative value in accounting for features of European Parliament elections. The following analysis deals largely with the central point at issue between the competing theories, the explanation of government losses. It deals only indirectly with turnout, in as much as differential turnout is essential to such explanations.

Explaining Government Vote Loss in European Parliament Elections

Much of the work on second order-elections has followed Reif and Schmitt (1980) in examining election results, using aggregate data. Regarding 2004, analyses have already been completed which indicate that the patterns of gains and losses in these elections are in line with those in the previous five sets of European Parliament elections (e.g. Marsh 2005; Schmitt 2005; Hix and Marsh 2007). The 'success' of second-order theory in this context is unsurprising and in line with previous work at this level, although it is evident that patterns in post-communist states are not quite the same as those in the older member states. This paper focuses on the individual level. This is more challenging as it brings into question not so much what is happening but who makes it happen. In particular we want to observe the pattern of voter mobility across the two elections (general to EP) and see how well it matches the expectations of the various theories already discussed. The approach follows previous work using the 1999 European election study (Marsh 2003, 2007).

Specific expectations, derived from the discussion above, are listed below:

- H1 That most of the change is away from the government (surge and decline: Campbell_1).
- H2 That government will lose more votes to non-voting than opposition parties (surge and decline: Campbell_1).
- H3 Independent voters are less likely to turn out at European elections than general elections, relative to partisans (surge and decline: Campbell_1).

- H4 Low interest voters are more likely to switch or abstain from government parties (surge and decline: Campbell_1).
- H5 There should be a higher defection of partisans at general elections than European elections (surge and decline: Campbell_1).
- H6 Opposition partisans who abstained last time will rejoin the opposition side (surge and decline: Campbell_2).
- H7 Weak opposition partisans who voted for the government last time will return to the opposition (surge and decline: Campbell_2).
- H8 There should be a shift away from the government by voters dissatisfied with its record (referendum).
- H9 Satisfied government supporters abstain more then dissatisfied ones who are more likely to switch (referendum).
- H10 Change and stability are a function of first-order concerns so left–right attitudes may affect decisions to switch or stay (second-order).
- H11 Second-order concerns are not relevant: i.e. European attitudes do not affect the decision of voters to switch (second-order).

Earlier work on the 1999 elections gave mixed results. Partisanship did matter in explaining voting patterns with defections more common in general elections, and non-partisans less likely to vote in EP elections, sustaining the sort of 'normal' vote interpretation of mid-term elections put forward by Cambell_1. Government popularity, however, proved a poor guide to defections and gave little support to the simple referendum interpretation of these elections. Second-order interpretations were supported in as much as patterns of vote switching were consistent with the view that some voters have multiple preferences: switchers have another option, abstainers do not. However, contrary to second-order theory, Europe did appear to matter, with government defectors significantly more critical about further integration than those who stayed loyal. This result is broadly in line with some recent aggregate studies suggesting anti-European parties and parties divided on Europe suffer in EP elections (Ferrara and Weishaupt 2004; Hix and Marsh 2007).

There are two particularly significant points of interest in the 2004 elections. The first is to see if the impact of European attitudes in 1999 was a quirk, or whether it is repeated and, if it is, whether or not it is strengthened. The latter might be expected, given the further erosion of the old 'permissive consensus' and the very visible success of anti-EU parties in a number of countries. The second is possible variation between old and new member states. This may have several sources. One is that party attachment might have a rather different meaning in new democracies and represent much more a short-term attraction than a long-term predisposition (e.g. Schmitt 2009). Another is that the very instability of party systems in many post-communist states hardly testifies to strong attachments and does not provide favourable conditions for the development of attachments (e.g. Sikk 2005). Of the ten new member states, only two are not new democracies and one of those is not included in the data used here.

Data for this paper are from the European Election Study 2004. About 27,000 interviews were carried out with electors just after the 2004 elections in all EU member states apart from Malta. Between 500 (in Cyprus) and 2,100 (in Sweden) electors responded to questionnaires, with an average of over 1,100 in each country. Country samples were weighted so that each sums to 1,000.[4]

Operationalizations are as follows:

- *Vote change*: differences between recalled vote at the last national election and reported EP vote.[5]
- *Partisanship*: feeling of being close to a party, measured on a four-point scale: not close, sympathiser, quite close, very close. This is coded from −3 (very close to opposition party) to +3 (very close to government party) with 'not close' as zero.
- *Government popularity*: approval or disapproval of the government's record to date, running from −1 (disapproval) through zero (don't know) to +1 (approval).
- *Views on Europe*: item on attitude to Unification which uses a 1–10-point scale to indicate whether integration has gone too far or should be pushed further. This is recoded here as a 10-point scale from −4.5 (too far) to +4.5 (further).
- *Left–right self-placement*: respondents were asked to place themselves on a 10-point left–right scale from 1 (left) to 10 (right).
- *Political interest*: four point scale of self-assessed interest in politics from none (0), a little (1), somewhat (2) to very (3). Missing values were coded 0.

Table 1 contains the evidence of voters' movements between the two elections, general (GE) and European (EP), showing in each case whether they voted for a government party, an opposition party, or did not vote. This provides a basis for evaluating the surge and decline hypotheses 1–2. We can see from Table 1 that the government parties lost a higher proportion of votes than did the opposition — retaining only 51 per cent of their GE votes as opposed to the opposition's 65 per cent, as would be expected under H1. However, we can also see that erstwhile government supporters are no more likely to abstain than are erstwhile opposition voters, in contrast to the expectation in H2. Shifts in aggregate support are not due to differential turnout. Amongst clear non-habitual voters, that is those who did not vote

Table 1. European Parliament election vote and recalled national election vote

National vote recall	Within-opposition change	EP vote recall			Within-govt change	Total
		Opposition	None	Govt		
Opposition	23	43	32	5		100
None		14	82	4		100
Government		17	30	44	9	100

Weighted for analysis to equalize country size. Analysis excludes Italy, Luxembourg, Northern Ireland, Malta, Czech Republic, Slovakia, Lithuania and Hungary.
Source: European Election Study 2004.

in the EP election, the government did marginally worse last time than the opposition (30 per cent of 9,069 as opposed to 30 per cent of 10,772: 31 per cent as against 37 per cent). The marginal figures indicate a small under-recall of government support here, although not enough to suggest government support from such voters was significantly higher in the general election. A rough adjustment of these figures to allow for errors in recall would still indicate that 2004 non-voters did not favour the government parties in the previous general election.

There are some differences here between new and old member states and it should be said that the under-recall of government voting is more severe in the new states: only 42 per cent of those who recalled voting in the general election claimed to have voted for the government but, in those elections, 48 per cent of voters did so.[6] In the old states, government parties kept 56 per cent of their votes compared to 39 per cent in the new states, while oppositions kept 72 per cent and 53 per cent, respectively. When it comes to the EP votes of GE abstainers, these clearly favour the opposition in both sets of countries by a ratio of 3: 1. In general, differences are slight but the new states did show more volatility.

In multi-party systems there is, of course, a switching of parties that is not apparent in Table 1: that between government parties or between opposition parties. In all, 26 per cent of stable government voters switched government party (24 per cent in the old countries, 32 per cent in the new ones) but 46 per cent of stable opposition voters did so; 72 per cent in the new accession states shifted opposition party. This is a remarkable degree of volatility across the two elections in the new member states.

Surge and decline theories direct most attention to the party attachments of voters, arguing that tendencies to stay, abstain or switch vary across different categories. Several of our hypotheses, including H3, H5, H6 and H7, deal with the differential behaviour of government and opposition partisans and of non-partisans. We thus need to know something of the character of the voters in the different cells. Table 2 makes this clearer, breaking down the voter transition matrix in Table 1 by party attachment, coded here as simply 'Opposition', 'None' and 'Government'.

H3 would lead us to expect that independents who voted for the government in the national election would be more likely to abstain in the European Parliament election, whereas partisans who crossed over should return. This is what we find. Of the independents who voted for the government last time, 39 per cent abstained in the European election and more stayed with the government (36 per cent) then switched (25 per cent). H6 and H7 deal with the behaviour of opposition partisans. Partisan defection was rare in the general election but of the tiny number of 'disadvantaged' partisans who defected to the government last time, 55 per cent returned, compared to only 14 per cent who stayed and 32 per cent who abstained. H6 predicts partisans of the non-government party should move from abstention back to their party. However, there are very few of them and, while 24 per cent returned, 67 per cent continued to abstain. H7 also suggests that independents should switch back from the government, but this was less common than abstention.

Table 2.   Recalled national vote by party attachment and European Parliament vote

National vote recall attached to ...	Within-opposition change	EP vote recall			Within-govt change	Total
		Opposition	None	Govt		
Opposition						
Opposition	22	52	25	2		100
Independent	26	32	35	7		100
Government	14	27	23	37		100
Total	23	43	29	4		100
None						
Opposition		30	69	2		100
Independent		11	86	4		100
Government		9	69	22		100
Total		14	82	5		100
Government						
Opposition		52	31	14	3	100
Independent		23	38	28	12	100
Government		8	24	61	7	100
Total		17	30	44	9	100

Cell entries are row percentages. *n* weighted to equalize country size. Analysis excludes Italy, Luxembourg, Northern Ireland, Malta, Czech Republic, Slovakia, Lithuania and Hungary.
Source: European Election Study 2004.

A further expectation from Campbell_1 (H5) is that there should be more defections — that is, those identifying with one party but voting for another — in general elections than in European ones. The numbers are very small here. Only 8 per cent of partisans who voted defected in the national election and 10 per cent in the European election. On the whole, these results suggests the original theory, Campbell_1 is more useful here than the revised one, Campbell_2, since there is little support for either H6 or H7 and more for H3 and H5.

These results hold generally true for both the old and new member states. Overall there seems to be very little difference in the patterns observed. Only with respect to the last point concerning the probability of defecting is there an interesting difference. Here we see that partisan defections are less common in national elections in the old member states (11 per cent in EP election, 6 per cent in the general election) but more common in national elections in the new accession states: 14 per cent as against 9 per cent. This pattern in the old states is the reverse of what was found in 1999, when general elections involved more defection, but, of course, overall the percentages are small.

While this detailed analysis is necessary to test some ideas of surge and decline theory, and to give some idea of the numbers involved, a more general and multivariate analysis is preferable to consider the other expectations.

Such an analysis also allows us to control for the country factor in our dataset. We are particularly interested in those voters in the first and third rows, those who voted for or against the government last time, and in how their behaviour in this 2004 election is related to characteristics like partisanship, satisfaction and their views on Europe.

Table 3 contains sets of coefficients that indicate the impact of a set of predictors on the probability of shifting or abstaining rather than staying with the government party (the reference option). Table 4 shows the impact of the same set of predictor variables on the probability of shifting or abstaining, rather than staying with the opposition party (the reference option). The cell entries are log odds ratios which show the average change in the odds of defection or abstention relative to stability, and the associated *p*-values. We can use these two tables as evidence in relation to the expectations outlined earlier, starting again with those from surge and decline theory.

As these results show, partisanship is linked significantly both to abstention and defection patterns, both in the case of previous government and non-government parties. For former government voters, as partisanship inclines towards the government it seems to have more impact on defection than abstention. The odds of defection from the government are more than halved with a one-point increase in attachment, whereas the odds of abstention drop a little less. Pro-government attachment also hugely raises the odds of defecting (back perhaps) from the opposition but, as we have seen, there are few such deviant government partisans. On interest (H4), it is apparent that more interested voters are about half as likely to abstain than stay or switch. This holds both for those who voted for government parties and for non-government parties in the previous general election.

H8 and H9 from referendum theories offer two different possibilities: that defection or abstention from the government is a function of approval (Tufte), and that abstention is not a function of approval, but that defection is (negative voting). Results give some support to referendum theory (H8), but suggest the weakness of negative voting theory (H9). Voters to leave the government when they are dissatisfied: the odds of doing so rather than staying increase by more than sixty points. However, there is no sign at all of negative voting, which would require a link between disapproval and switching but not between disapproval and abstention. The coefficients are quite similar and equally significant.

Second-order theory rests on the assumption that voters have preferences across a number of parties and that different elections provide different contexts in which they select from their set. However, it suggests that voters will be motivated by first-order issues rather than second-order ones. This is a difficult thing to test but we make a start here by comparing the impact on defection and abstention of two general sets of issues: those relating to European integration and those relating to the left–right dimension. In each case we have taken the simplest specification, asking whether the left–right and pro-/anti-integration position have anything to do with defection. The results appear to show that a voter's views on the EU are not connected to the probability of changing party blocs but are related to abstention. This

Table 3. Factors explaining EP choices of general election supporters of government parties: multinomial logit estimates (odds ratios)

	Within government change			Opposition change			Abstained		
	All	Old-15	New-10	All	Old-15	New-10	All	Old-15	New-10
Government approval	0.75	0.71	0.94	0.53	0.56	0.5	0.61	0.65	0.51
	0.000	*0.000*	*0.742*	*0.000*	*0.000*	*0.000*	*0.000*	*0.000*	*0.000*
Positive attitude to EU	1.26	1.34	0.97	0.9	0.88	0.86	0.61	0.62	0.56
	0.016	*0.007*	*0.927*	*0.116*	*0.097*	*0.417*	*0.000*	*0.000*	*0.000*
Left–right (10-point scale)	1.18	1.2	1.15	1.03	0.96	1.24	1.01	0.63	1.56
	0.000	*0.000*	*0.009*	*0.063*	*0.062*	*0.000*	*0.595*	*0.000*	*0.001*
Pro-govt attachment (7-point scale)	0.57	0.55	0.55	0.35	0.39	0.26	0.57	0.95	0.44
	0.000	*0.000*	*0.000*	*0.000*	*0.000*	*0.000*	*0.000*	*0.008*	*0.000*
Political interest (4-point scale)	1.02	1.02	0.98	0.77	0.77	0.73	1.36	1.38	1.27
	0.759	*0.675*	*0.915*	*0.000*	*0.000*	*0.000*	*0.000*	*0.000*	*0.022*
Observations	5,856	4,774	1,082						
Pseudo-R^2	0.11	0.09	0.20						

Country dummies included but not shown; *p*-values in italics. Reference category is support for government parties in EP election. Analysis excludes Italy, Luxembourg, Northern Ireland, Malta, Czech Republic, Slovakia, Lithuania and Hungary.

Table 4. Factors explaining EP choices of general election supporters of opposition parties: multinomial logit estimates (odds ratios)

	Within government change			Opposition change			Abstained		
	All	Old-15	New-10	All	Old-15	New-10	All	Old-15	New-10
Government approval	0.96	0.85	1.42	1.81	1.62	2.90	0.95	0.97	1.00
	0.304	*0.001*	*0.000*	*0.000*	*0.000*	*0.000*	*0.272*	*0.493*	*0.987*
Positive attitude to EU	0.90	0.83	1.24	1.05	1.04	1.25	0.62	0.62	0.70
	0.044	*0.001*	*0.108*	*0.664*	*0.738*	*0.426*	*0.000*	*0.000*	*0.000*
Left–right (10-point scale)	0.95	0.88	0.98	1.07	1.03	0.90	0.97	0.96	0.97
	0.000	*0.000*	*0.531*	*0.013*	*0.002*	*0.208*	*0.051*	*0.020*	*0.003*
Pro-govt attachment (7-point scale) government	1.50	1.57	1.53	3.56	3.30	3.47	1.48	1.43	1.60
	0.000	*0.000*	*0.000*	*0.000*	*0.000*	*0.000*	*0.000*	*0.000*	*0.000*
Political interest (4-point scale)	1.01	0.99	1.02	1.02	0.95	1.27	1.66	1.63	1.69
	0.816	*0.814*	*0.878*	*0.000*	*0.549*	*0.311*	*0.000*	*0.000*	*0.000*
Observations	5,856	5,036	1,238						
Pseudo-R^2	0.08	0.08	0.11						

Country dummies included but not shown; *p*-values in italics. Reference category is support for opposition parties in EP election. Analysis excludes Italy, Luxembourg, Northern Ireland, Malta, Czech Republic, Slovakia, Lithuania and Hungary gives some support to H10. A one-point increase in support for integration is associated with a significant drop in the odds of abstention but not of defection. This is not a strong relationship but it is consistent across erstwhile government and opposition supporters. In contrast, left–right position does appear to have an impact on switching as well as defection, particularly for erstwhile government supporters. In other words, pro-EU voters are more likely to vote, but left-wing voters are more likely to switch.

These results generally hold true consistently across the old and new member states but there are exceptions, most notably with respect to the attitude dimensions. Left–right orientations are linked more consistently to abstention in the new states, particularly amongst those who voted for opposition parties last time. Left–right orientations (i.e. being more left wing) are linked more closely to defection in the old states: erstwhile government voters are about one-quarter less likely to defect when they are one point more right wing, a change which makes erstwhile opposition voters about one quarter more likely to defect. There are also differences with respect to party attachment which seems a stronger determinant of stability in the new member states. A one-point increase in attachment to a government party is associated with a change in the odds of staying of about 3: 1 in the new states as opposed to less than 2: 1 in the old ones among erstwhile government supporters; among erstwhile opposition supporters the odds of changing increase by over 4: 1 as opposed to about 2: 1.

In two further pieces of analysis we explored the importance of voters' relative utilities for different parties, replicating analysis of 1999 (Marsh 2003, 2007) as well as exploring the volatility within the opposition parties. First, using the party utility measures developed by van der Eijk (Tillie 1995; van der Eijk and Franklin 1996), we examined how the distance between the highest utility for a government party and the highest utility for an opposition party impacted on voters' decisions to switch, abstain or remain loyal. This analysis was kept separate because of the much greater degree of missing data on these questions, the overall *n* for analysis dropping by about 30 per cent. This variable proves to have a strong impact on vote choice. Government voters who perceive a positive differential between the two sets of parties are much less likely to defect, and less likely to abstain; similarly, opposition voters who perceive a differential are more likely to defect and abstain. In each case the effects on switching are much greater than those on abstention. The inclusion of this variable leaves the relative importance of other variables, and conclusions drawn above, unchanged. But it does indicate the possibility that voters do consider a number of parties in the vote choice set and, where differentials are small, may change their vote decision from election to election.

Volatility within the opposition parties — a topic not envisaged by US midterm election theories — is best explained by party attachment, but political interest and attitudes to the EU play a small part: those more interested are more likely to remain loyal, as are those more pro-EU, although both coefficients are significant only at the 0.05 level. Those who switch within the set of government parties are simply less partisan. These relationships, particular within new member states, will be explored further in a later version of this paper.

Discussion

This paper has examined the expectations we might have about the 2004 elections in the light of available theoretical work both on European Parliament elections and the analogous US mid-term elections. We contrasted the US-based theories of Angus Campbell and his successors with Reif and Schmitt's theory of second-order elections on the basis that all seek to explain the comparable patterns of regularity in different political systems. There are differences between the theories. These lie chiefly in different conceptions of what motivates the average voter, with surge and decline allowing for more strategic, 'rational' behaviour than the other theories, but they also lie in the behaviour that each was developed to explain. Surge and decline and referendum theories focus on behaviour in a two-party system with a separation of powers and an electorate that is easily categorized as identifying with one party or another. In parliamentary democracies none of these conditions applies. Two-party systems are rare, even if they are liberally defined; there is no separation of powers, and party identification — as the concept is understood in the USA — is much less easily separated from immediate voting intentions. Nonetheless, the assumption with which this paper began was that such theories are at least potentially applicable in the different circumstances. Second-order election theory has grown out of this literature but offers explanations for matters outside the normal ambit of US-focused studies, such as the shift of votes from larger to smaller parties, as well as adapting previous insights to understanding electoral change in sub- and supra-national elections.

On the whole we discovered all three areas of theory do offer some understanding of the mechanics of individual vote change. The expectations derived from surge and decline theory are only confirmed in part by the data. First, there is mixed evidence that government losses can be seen as a consequence of voters returning to 'normal' behaviour. While defections do not appear to be much greater in European elections, it seems that defections by partisans were not significantly more apparent in general elections than European elections, a finding that runs counter to some popular wisdom that European elections are contexts in which partisanship counts for little. We also see at the individual level that independent voters are more likely than others to abstain at the lower stimulus election and that partisanship is linked to shifts in and out of the voting public in some of the expected ways, although it is evident that 'peripheral' voters alone are not responsible for the losses suffered by governments. It must be acknowledged that these findings may be distorted by the fact that we have only recall evidence for the last national election We badly need widespread panel data on these elections, something that is not yet available for more than the odd country (e.g. Heath et al. 1999). Even so, the distortions in recall might be expected to strengthen links between partisanship and recalled choice rather than weaken them and the evidence here should certainly not be discounted on that point. In general the findings give more value to Campbell's original formulation that his namesake's revised version. While not every expectation is fulfilled, not all can be dismissed.

Traditional referendum theory gets some support. The individual-level analysis revealed modest results with respect to government popularity but it is clear that this factor does help to explain voting shifts.[7]

Evidence with respect to the attitudes of voters, a focus prompted by second-order theory again was mixed. As expected, attitudes to the EU do not seem to account for vote switching between government and opposition. In contrast left–right orientations do help account for such changes, with left-wing voters more inclined to shift towards or stay loyal to opposition parties. However, abstention by general election voters does seem to be more common among less pro-EU voters. These results are based on rather crude measures and more sophisticated specifications are certainly possible. Governments in general tend to be favourable to integration: we would therefore expect opposition voters to be motivated more by anti- than by pro-integrationist views. An alternative specification, using a voter's close-ness to the EU position of the government [mean position of government parties as seen by all voters] gave very similar results. We also explored other specifications for left–right, including a moderate–extremist folding of the left–right scale. Arguably, most governments are centrist and the opposition should attract more extremist voters (or they might go to more 'outspoken' coalition (or opposition) parties). There was some support for this, but the unfolded scale was considerably more powerful and we opted for simplicity. Second-order theory suggests voters will opt for the closest party on the major dimensions on national politics. This specification will be tested in a subsequent version of this paper.

There are some contrasts here with a similar analysis using data on the 1999 elections. In particular, the traditional referendum theory is much better supported here, and the signs that the EU mattered to government defections is now absent. However, the relevance of surge and decline theory and the patterns of change by party attachment are very similar. There are also some contrasts between patterns in the new and old member states — essentially between the new and the older democracies, although for the most part the picture is quite similar. There was more volatility in the new member states, and partisanship seems to be less of a constraint on vote choice. Differences are also apparent with respect to the values underlying switching. The link between being more anti-EU and abstaining in EP elections, and between being more left-wing and defecting from government parties is significant only in the old member states.

This paper has focused largely on a review of theories of lower stimulus elections, exploring differences and similarities between them, in order to assess what each can tell us about European Parliament elections. Most offer something of value, although some have a wider potential than others. What we can say is that we certainly did not lack useful tools for generating expec-tations about the 2004 elections and for analysing them in retrospect. We have shown several clear patterns in previous results, many of them quite consistent with theory and thus interpretable in such terms. We have also reported on many similarities between the old and new member states in respect to the dynamics of change, although volatility in the new states remains much higher than in the old states. Moreover, certain types of volatility — that within the sets of parties in government or in opposition — is not envisaged by theories of surge and decline or 'referendums', but might be in accordance with second-order theory regarding the differential prospects of large and small parties. Weak party attachment seems to be a factor in all of this, but more work needs to be done to explore the precise patterns of within-camp changes.

Acknowledgement

The author wishes to express his gratitude to the TCD Arts and Social Sciences Benefaction Fund and to Jane Suiter for research assistance on this paper.

Notes

1. Second-order elections theory can be seen as an early exploration in the then-uncharted territory of multi-level governance (e.g. Hooghe and Marks 2001).
2. As the policy reach of multi-level governance grows within the EU an increasingly large body of issues is dealt with in both first- and second-order political arenas (see again Hooghe and Marks 2001, appendix table 1). What is referred to here is therefore the specifics of the national and the European arena, which is the political standing of the national government on the one hand, and the future direction of European integration — whether one should speed it up or slow it down — on the other.
3. For a concise review of some other variants, see Campbell (1993).
4. Full details on EES website: http://www.ees-homepage.net.
5. An alternative operationalization would be to contrast the EP vote with vote in a hypothetical general election at the same time. This was used by Oppenhuis, van der Eijk, and Franklin (1996). It has the advantage of removing the bias of recall data but the disadvantage of being subject to the same second-order effects of any opinion poll taken between elections. However, Oppenhuis, van der Eijk, and Franklin's findings on the existence of switching and abstention contributing to government party losses are similar to those in the analysis here (below).
6. The error is seven percentage points in the EP elections: the survey shows 30 per cent as against a target figure of 37 per cent. Corresponding figures for the older member states are 0 per cent for the general election vote and −2 for the EP election vote.
7. Mixed results have also been found in the US context: see Niemi and Weisberg (1993, 209).

References

Campbell, A. 1960. Surge and decline: A study of electoral change. *Public Opinion Quarterly* 24: 397–418.

Campbell, A. 1966. Surge and decline: A study of electoral change. In *Elections and the political order*, eds. A. Campbell, P. Converse, W. Miller and D. Stokes, 40–62. New York: Wiley.

Campbell, J.E. 1993. *The presidential pulse of congressional elections.* Lexington: Univ. Press of Kentucky.

Ferrara, Federico, and J. Timo Weishaupt. 2004. Get your act together: Party performance in European Parliament elections. *European Union Politics* 5, no. 3: 283–306.

Heath, Adrian, Iain McLean, Bridget Taylor, and John Curtice. 1999. Between first and second order: A comparison of voting behaviour in European and local elections in Britain. *European Journal of Political Research* 35, no. 3: 389–414.

Hix, S., and M. Marsh. 2007. Punishment or protest? Understanding European Parliament elections. *Journal of Politics* 69, no. 3: 495–510.

Hooghe, L., and G. Marks. 2001. *Multi-level governance and European integration.* Lanham, MD: Rowman & Littlefield.

Kernell, S. 1977. Presidential popularity and negative voting: An alternative explanation of the midterm congressional decline of the President's party. *American Political Science Review* 71: 44–66.

Marsh, M. 2003. Theories of less important elections: Explanations of electoral behaviour in European Parliament elections. *Revue de la Maison francaise d'Oxford* 1, no. 1: 189–210.

Marsh, M. 2005. The results of the 2004 European Parliament elections and the second-order model. In *Europawahl 2004,* eds. O. Niedermayer and H. Schmitt, 142–58. Wiesbaden: Verlag für Sozialwissenschaften.

Marsh, M. 2007. What happens in European Parliament elections? In *Voting in European Parliament elections: Lessons from the past and scenarios for the future,* eds. Cees Van der Eijk and Wouter Van der Brug, 51–72. Indiana: Univ. of Notre Dame Press.

Niemi, R., and R. Weisberg, eds. 1993. *Controversies in voting behavior,* 3rd edn. Washington, DC: CQ Press.

Oppenhuis, E.V., C. van der Eijk, and M. Franklin. 1996. The party context: Outcomes. In *Choosing Europe? The European electorate and national politics in the face of union,* eds. C. Van der Eijk and M. Franklin, 287–305. Ann Arbor: The Univ. of Michigan Press.

Reif, K. 1985. National electoral cycles and European elections 1979 and 1984. *Electoral Studies* 3: 244–55.

Reif, K. 1997. European elections as member state second-order elections revisited. *European Journal of Political Research* 31, nos 1–2: 115–24.

Reif, K., and H. Schmitt. 1980. Nine second-order national elections. A conceptual framework for the analysis of European election results. *European Journal of Political Research* 8: 3–44.

Schmitt, H. 2005. The European Parliament elections of June 2004: Still second-order?. *West European Politics* 28: 650–79.

Schmitt, H. 2009. Multiple party identifications. In *The comparative study of electoral systems,* ed. H.-D. Klingemann, 137–57. Oxford: Oxford Univ. Press.

Sikk, A. 2005. How unstable? Volatility and the genuinely new parties in Eastern Europe. *European Journal of Political Research* 44: 391–412.

Tillie, J. 1995. *Party utility and voting behaviour.* Amsterdam: Het Spinhuis.

Tufte, E.R. 1975. Determinants of the outcomes of midterm congressional elections. *American Political Science Review* 67: 540–54.

Van der Eijk, C., and Mark Franklin et al. 1996. *Choosing Europe? The European electorate in the face of unification.* Ann Arbor: Univ. of Michigan Press.

Second-Order Elections versus First-Order Thinking: How Voters Perceive the Representation Process in a Multi-Layered System of Governance

NICK CLARK* & ROBERT ROHRSCHNEIDER**

*Department of Political Science, Indiana University, Bloomington, USA; **Department of Political Science, University of Kansas, Lawrence, USA

ABSTRACT   Second-order election models are based on several assumptions about individual-level motivations. These can be summarized by a *transfer hypothesis*: individuals presumably apply their evaluations of national-level phenomena to the EU level when voting in EU elections. In contrast, a *suis generis* hypothesis stipulates that voters evaluate the EU on its own performance terms. This paper tests these competing hypotheses. We find considerable support for both models. In the election context, where national institutions — political parties — dominate the representation process, the transfer hypothesis receives considerable support. However, we also find surprisingly strong support for the first-order hypothesis: electoral choice in EU election is influenced to a considerable extent by EU level factors. Furthermore, when voters evaluate the mechanisms of representation more broadly without a focus on elections *per se*, we find much more support for the first-order than the transfer hypothesis — voters clearly separate the two levels and evaluate each level on its own terms. These results have important implications, both for how we analyse voters' decisions in European elections, and how we view the sophistication of voters more broadly in the context of multi-layered institutions.

Correspondence Address: Nick Clark, 1100 E. 7th St., Department of Political Science, Indiana University, Bloomington, IN 47405, USA. E-mail: nijclark@indiana.edu

Robert Rohrschneider, 1541 Lilac Lane–504 Blake, Department of Political Science, University of Kansas, Lawrence, KS, 66044, USA. E-mail: roro@ku.edu

Introduction

The EU's democracy deficit — the presumed inability of the EU to represent citizens — is becoming an increasing concern to analysts and observers of the European Union (Majone 1998; Schmitt and Thomassen 1999; Rohrschneider 2002). A key element of the presumed deficit is that elections are not evaluations of the EU's performance *per se* but mostly reflect voters' judgements about national political issues (Reif 1980; Marsh 1998; Hix and Marsh 2007). Consistent with this argument, legions of studies provide evidence supporting this interpretation: the national economy influences EU election outcomes, government parties lose vote shares in EU elections, especially during the mid-term of a parliamentary cycle, smaller and extremist parties usually gain in EU-wide elections, and turnout in European elections is substantially lower than in national elections (Reif and Schmitt 1980; Hix and Marsh 2007; van der Brug, van der Eijk, and Franklin 2007). Because EU elections are presumably dominated by events at the national level, they are dubbed 'second-order' elections.

This interpretation of EU elections makes several assumptions, key of which is the premise that national considerations dominate voters' decisions even in EU elections. Voters presumably rely on the popularity of national governments to decide whom to support in EU elections; they rely on the national economy to allocate their support accordingly, and so on. Because voters presumably transfer their perceptions of national events to the EU level, we will refer to this individual-level mechanism as the *transfer* hypothesis.

In light of the transfer hypothesis, it is surprising how few analyses directly examine the extent to which perceptions of national- versus EU-level factors influence the party preferences of voters. As we will detail below, the vast majority of studies rely on an aggregate approach, with all its promises and pitfalls. Analysts have only recently begun to directly examine the transfer hypothesis at the individual level (Carrubba and Timpone 2005; Schmitt 2005; Schmitt, Sanz, and Braun 2008). All in all, however, we know little about the reasons for voters' electoral choice in a multi-layered system of governance.

This gap in our knowledge is unfortunate because there actually are several reasons why one might plausibly argue that voters increasingly evaluate the EU *sui generis*. For one, the EU has become more important over time to individual citizens, certainly since the Maastricht and Amsterdam treaties came into force in the 1990s. An increasing number of laws are passed by the EU, which means that the decisions taken by the EU affect a growing number of citizens. What is more, European integration has moved beyond economics — which was widely carried by a permissive consensus — to politics which is based on a 'restrained dissent', in Hooghe and Marks' (2008) words. As a result, citizens may increasingly rely on their preferences about European integration *per se*, as well as their perceptions of the EU's performance or that of the performance of national parties at the EU level, when they cast a ballot in EU elections or more generally judge the representation process at the EU level. Thus, in contrast to the transfer hypothesis, this *suis generis* hypothesis expresses the idea that citizens arrive at voting decisions in EU elections and judge the EU on the basis of EU-related factors.

This paper, then, contributes to the growing body of research by analysing the validity of the *transfer* and *sui generis* hypotheses. We will proceed as follows. First, we will examine the extent to which citizens rely on national versus EU-based performance indicators in European elections. This is necessary because the transfer hypothesis is directly tailored to the nature of European elections. Secondly, we will broaden the analyses to examine how citizens generally evaluate the process of representation at the national and EU levels. We deem this necessary because we would like to examine whether the *transfer* and *suis generis* hypotheses can be generalized to the EU more broadly.

The Individual-Level Foundation of Second-Order Elections Models

What are the key elements of the second-order election model? The main evidence for this model consists of four observations (Reif and Schmitt 1980; Hix and Marsh 2007). First, compared to national elections, voters typically defect from government parties in European elections. This is consistent with the observation that large parties, who are likely to be included in national governments, tend to lose votes in European elections when compared to the last national elections. Secondly, smaller parties tend to increase their vote share from the last national election to a subsequent EU election. Thirdly, this defection from larger to smaller parties is *especially* pronounced during the middle of parliamentary cycles. This is consistent with the observation that the extent of parties' vote gains and losses is mediated by the national electoral cycle at the time EU elections take place. Finally, turnout rates at national elections are significantly higher than participation rates in EU elections. Cumulatively, this evidence seems to indicate that voters transfer information from the performance of national party systems to the EU level.

The second-order election model is not only supported empirically, it also makes a lot of sense from the perspective of party competition. For one, political parties in most European countries are ordered along a left–right division within nation-states. Given this programmatic commitment at the level of nation-states, they have few incentives to go against their programmatic tradition in EU-wide elections (Andeweg 1995; Gabel 2000). This, in turn, severely restricts citizens' ability to evaluate the EU *sui generis* since parties are the key representatives at both levels. Thus, unless an EU-related issue cuts across the left–right dimension, which increases a party's capacity to develop stances that are not tied to its programmatic heritage, it is hard to see how parties can ignore their programmatic heritage in EU elections. In short, they must — indeed should — connect their stances about integration to their domestic policies in order to maintain their credibility. For these reasons, students of party positions on European integration find that parties' left–right stances on domestic cleavages strongly predict their integration stances (Dalton 2005; Marks et al. 2006; Rohrschneider and Whitefield 2007). Thus, the institutionalized role of national political parties in EU elections reinforces citizens' inclinations to transfer information from the national level to that of the EU. Finally, further reinforcing the transfer hypothesis is the fact that analyses about EU support show that the popularity of national governments is taken as a proxy of how well the EU performs and, subsequently, affects citizens' evaluations of the European Union (Anderson 1998). This too suggests that individuals transfer information from the level of nation-states to the level of the EU.

All in all, there exist both conceptual reasons and considerable empirical evidence in support of the transfer hypothesis. However, while the transfer hypothesis is plausible, it is not the only mechanism that might underlie these results.

Problems of Second-Order Models

Despite the widespread support for second-order models, we actually know fairly little about the extent to which voters behave in EU elections according to perceptions of national factors. The gap in our knowledge mainly results from the focus of most second-order elections models on aggregate election outcomes. This is somewhat surprising given that the logic of the argument attributes special importance to the perceptions of individuals in deciding how to cast their ballot at the national and supranational levels. Let us consider why the focus on aggregate data alone does not produce the kind of evidence needed to test the transfer and *suis generis* hypotheses.

The dependent variable is typically the vote loss/gain for each party, when election outcomes in national and supranational elections are compared. The change scores are then correlated with variables measuring party characteristics (e.g. party size; government status, etc.). Given this aggregate approach, however, it remains unclear precisely why voters defect from governmental parties. For many patterns found at the aggregate level are actually consistent with both the transfer and *suis generis* hypothesis. For example, small party support in EU elections is often taken as a sign that voters defect from large government parties because of their performance as a governing party. As Hix and Marsh (2007, 22) put it, 'the main story is that "party size" matters, as the second-order model predicts. Small parties gain and large parties ... lose'. This is no doubt the case in the aggregate, but what does this imply for how voters arrive at their decision to support a smaller party in an EU election over a larger party in a national election? The second-order model interprets this pattern as evidence that voters are dissatisfied with the performance of major parties in the national arena. This is clearly one possibility. However, another one — equally plausible we argue — is an interpretation that voters view both institutional layers separately, and apply different criteria in their decision making at each level: in our example, smaller parties (such as the Greens) may be supported in an EU election because they are perceived to do a better job in pushing green issues than larger parties would do at the EU level (Carrubba and Timpone 2005). Thus, while EP elections are no doubt less relevant in the consequences for the actual distribution of power, they may not be second-order in terms of the mechanisms that underlie the choice of voters. The aggregate approach is here running the danger of committing the ecological fallacy.

Another problem is the empirical focus of most second-order analyses on vote *switching* across the two levels. While the conceptual model itself speaks to both why voters defect from government parties (e.g. dissatisfaction with parties in government) or stay with them (e.g. satisfaction), the method entails that the analyses exclusively examine vote switching. Imagine a hypothetical scenario where all parties at the national and EU-level receive exactly the same aggregate vote share. In this case, there would be no variance across the two elections, and thus nothing could be explained with an aggregate model where parties' vote gains and losses constitute the dependent variable. These aggregate models only have an opportunity to explain gains and losses once net switching is greater than zero. In other words, the results of aggregate analyses are driven by (net) vote changes. The important point here is, then, that the way the dependent variable is designed does not use information about consistent vote choices across the two levels.

This shortcoming is unfortunate for at least two reasons. Conceptually, it is worth knowing why voters support the same parties at both levels or oppose them at both levels. For the transfer hypothesis assumes that voters are happy with the performance of parties at the national level if voters support government parties at the EU level. It is equally plausible that voters are happy with parties' performance at the EU level, independent of their performance at the national level. In addition, since consistency in party support is the norm, the aggregate approach of most second-order analyses focuses on the instances that constitute an empirical minority, ignoring evidence from the majority of voters who support or oppose the same parties at both levels.

To be clear, we do not suggest that the transfer hypothesis never applies. We suspect (though do not know for certain) that this is how many voters arrived at decisions during early European elections when the powers of the European Parliament were more restricted than they are now (Reif and Schmitt 1980). We also expect, however, that voters begin to evaluate the EU on its own terms given the growing importance of EU institutions in the policy-making process at the national level (Schmitt 2005, 654) and an increasing shift in the EU's focus from economic integration to more controversial proposals of political integration (Hooghe and Marks 2008). Neither do we argue that the transfer hypothesis is obsolete. However, we do suggest that it is an empirical question to determine the extent to which the transfer and *suis generis* mechanisms underlie voters' electoral choice in EU elections. We therefore see a need to examine the individual-level assumptions of the second-order model, in part because of the changing character of European integration, in part because the two mechanisms have not been systematically examined.

Hypotheses

We focus the analyses in this paper on the determinants of citizens' choice after they have decided to participate in an election.[1] In this context, the transfer hypothesis predicts:

> Hypothesis 1: Voters' performance evaluations of the national government and the national economy influence the extent to which voters defect from governmental parties in EU elections.

And, the following prediction is implied but has not been tested by most second-order models:

> Hypothesis 2: Voters' performance evaluations of the national government and the national economy influence the extent to which voters support the same party at the national and EU levels.

The *suis generis* hypothesis, in turn, predicts that vote choices at the EU level are made on the basis of EU-related factors. Specifically,

> Hypothesis 3: The perceived performance of parties at the EU level influences the extent to which voters defect from government parties.

> Hypothesis 4: Voters' performance evaluations of parties at the EU level influence the extent to which voters stay with the same party at the EU level.

Results

Our dependent variable in these analyses follows Carruba and Timbone (2005, 266). We created a new variable, based on voters' recalled past vote in the last national and EU elections. This new variable contains four cells: (1) voters support government parties in both elections; (2) support opposition parties in both elections; (3) move from government parties in national election to the opposition in EU elections; (4) defect from the opposition in national elections to (national) government parties in EU elections.[2]

We use the 1999 European Election Study which contains several performance indicators needed to test the hypotheses. We included two predictors located at the national level: public perceptions of the national economy and mass evaluations of the performance of national governments. The transfer hypothesis predicts that greater satisfaction with the economy and the national governments increases the odds that voters support governmental parties in both elections.

In contrast to most prior studies, however, we also included two predictors located at the EU level. One indicator measures voters' evaluations of the performance of parties at the EU level. This variable, while focused on national parties, attempts to gauge separately the perception of how well parties handle EU affairs.[3] Another variable measures citizens' support for European integration. (All measures are described in detail in Appendix A–C.)

Table 1. Predicting support for government parties across national/EP elections

	Electoral choices		
	Defections to opposition parties in EP elections	Defections to government parties in EP elections	Support for opposition parties across elections
Parties' government performance	−0.41**	−0.36**	−0.76**
	(0.11)	(0.07)	(0.09)
Economic perceptions	−0.23	−0.07	−0.23*
	(0.13)	(0.11)	(0.1)
Integration support	0.04	−0.53**	−0.28**
	(0.09)	(0.14)	(0.05)
Parties' EU performance	−0.06	−0.15*	−0.16**
	(0.05)	(0.06)	(0.04)
Strength of party attachment	−0.28	−1.03**	−0.18
	(0.4)	(0.28)	(0.19)
Far-left ideology	−0.53*	0.22	−0.38
	(0.24)	(0.21)	(0.39)
Left-centre ideology	−0.21	0.26	−0.44
	(0.25)	(0.23)	(0.34)
Right-centre ideology	0.28	0.35	0.53**
	(0.26)	(0.18)	(0.16)
Right ideology	−0.23	0.06	0.61*
	(0.35)	(0.18)	(0.26)
Far-right ideology	−0.56	−0.13	(0.71)
	(0.4)	(0.27)	(0.36)
Age	0.01**	0.01**	0.01*
	(0.003)	(0.003)	(0.005)
Education	0.02**	0.01*	0.01
	(0.006)	(0.006)	(0.007)
Sex	−0.05	−0.01	−0.26**
	(0.11)	(0.12)	(0.04)

Entries are coefficients from a multi-nominal logit analysis. Government supporters at both elections are the reference category.
*, ** significance at the 0.05 and 0.01 level, respectively. European weight is used.
Source: 1999 European Election Survey (5,997 observations).

Since the four levels of the dependent variable constitute a nominal variable, we conducted a multi-nominal logit analysis. Table 1 shows the coefficients, with government supporters at both levels serving as the reference category. The first column shows the coefficients for respondents who switch from governmental parties in national elections to opposition parties in the EU election. We note, first, that parties' governmental performance is a highly significant predictor, which clearly supports the transfer hypothesis. Those voters who are dissatisfied with the way the government performs are more likely to switch their support to an opposition party at the EU level. Also note that a perception that parties do well at the EU level does not induce voters to move from governmental to opposition parties. All of this is consistent with the transfer hypothesis — greater dissatisfaction with the perceived performance of national governments increases the odds of defection from governments to opposition parties in EU elections, while the performance of parties at the EU level seems irrelevant for voters who move from a government party in national elections to an opposition party at the EU level. However, we do note that when the governmental performance variable is dropped from the model, the EU performance variable becomes significant. This suggests that the transfer mechanism is connected to the fact that EU-wide elections are conducted through national party systems, and not a genuine, EU-wide party system (Andeweg 1995).

Turning to the group of voters who switch their vote from an opposition party in national elections to a government party in an EU election (column 2), we now note that the two EU predictors are statistically significant. First, when voters believe that parties do a good job at the EU level, they are more likely to move *towards* national government parties at the EU level. Remarkably, this pattern emerges regardless of their evaluations of governmental parties' performance in the national arena. Note also that supporters of integration are also more likely to switch towards governmental parties. This constitutes clear evidence in support of the *suis generis* hypothesis because voters move towards governmental parties not only when they are happy with the performance of governments — which does matter, as the first coefficient in the column indicates — but also because they perceive these parties to perform well at the EU level. Similarly, when voters support the EU *per se*, they are also more likely to switch from national opposition to supporting governmental parties in EU elections, perhaps because they would like to strengthen the role played by these parties in EU negotiations.[4] One possible explanation for this pattern may be that as the governing parties appoint representatives in the Council of Ministers; voters might be assigning greater responsibility for EU issues to governing parties.

Finally, support for all four hypotheses emerges from the last group of voters (column 3), which compares persistent government supporters to those who consistently oppose governmental parties. Here all performance predictors are statistically significant. Clearly, one reason for supporting opposition parties at both levels is that citizens are dissatisfied with national governments, both their performance and the national economy. But another reason is that if citizens disapprove of parties' performance at the EU level *per se*, then they are more likely to oppose the government at both levels. This not only means that the vote choice in EU elections is connected to perceptions of parties' EU level performance, but may also signal that the vote choice in national elections is affected to some degree by how parties perform at the EU level. Given that we control for partisanship, ideology and several nation-level performance perceptions, the significance of the EU-level performance variable seems to suggest that voters' decision to support opposition parties at both levels is related partly to their concerns with EU affairs. This interpretation is supported by the fact that general support for integration also affects the odds of supporting opposition parties in both arenas.

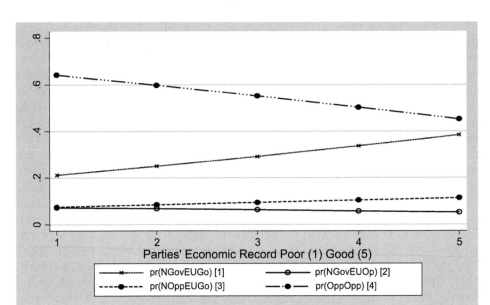

Figure 1.   National economic performance.

In order to convey a better sense of the predictive relevance of each variable, we plotted the predicted value of falling into one of the four categories against the theoretically relevant predictors (Figures 1, 2). The first two figures illustrate the impact of parties' economic record and perceived government

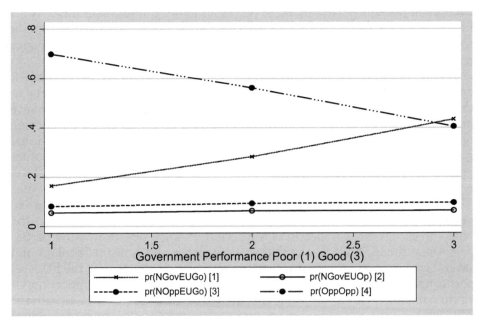

Figure 2.   Government performance.

performance on whether voters support governmental or opposition parties in both elections or exhibit cross-level defections. As expected, these graphs provide considerable support for the transfer hypothesis because they visualize the influence of national performance factors on EU-level vote choices.

Figures 3 and 4, however, show the impact of EU-related performance factors on vote choices. Visually, these are related less strongly to vote choices than evaluations of parties' government performance. At the same time, they do matter. In fact, parties' EU-based performance factors are nearly as important as national economic performance. For example, when perceptions move from being very dissatisfied with parties at the EU level, the probability of moving from national governments to an opposition party at the EU level are slightly above $p=0.20$. In contrast, when they are happy with the EU-level performance of parties, this nearly doubles to a probability of about $p=0.39$.

All in all, this evidence provides not only support for the transfer hypothesis, but for the *suis generis* hypothesis as well.

East–West Differences in Second-Order Elections?

Recent analyses have suggested that the second-order election model does not appear to be supported in new democracies in east-central Europe (Schmitt 2005; Koepke and Ringe 2006; Hix and Marsh 2007). This conclusion is based on the observation that the predictors of aggregate vote changes from national to EU elections in the west do not apply to the east. This nonfinding is consistent with evidence that national elections in new east-central European democracies demonstrate a much higher level of volatility between

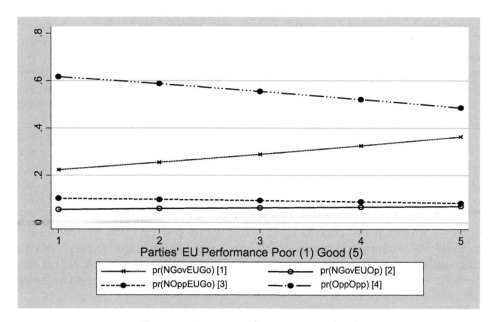

Figure 3.   Parties' performance at EU level.

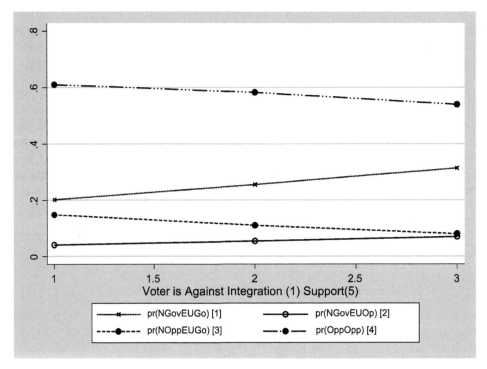

Figure 4. Support for European integration.

elections than in Western Europe (Tavits 2005; Caramani 2006); this volatility presumably undermines the development of a connection between
national and EU-level elections. The reason appears to be that east-central
Europeans do not link their performance evaluations as clearly to government and opposition parties as voters in the west, presumably because the
organizational and programmatic instability in the first fifteen years after the
democratic transition makes it difficult for voters to identify those parties
most likely to solve a problem — or to be responsible for it. Consequently,
the second-order model may not be applicable in east-central Europe.

   As argued in the previous section, however, we would suggest that it is
premature on the basis of aggregate change scores alone to characterize the
motives of individual voters. So in order to analyse the degree to which the
transfer and *suis generis* hypotheses do not apply to new democracies, we
conducted a tentative analysis of vote changes across national and EU elections. Naturally, the 1999 European Election Study does not cover the
newer democracies of central and Eastern Europe (CEE) that joined the EU
in 2004. We therefore use the 2004 European Election Study, even though
this study lacks a few important variables, notably one that measures the
performance of parties at the EU level. The following analyses are therefore
of a preliminary character.

   We first constructed the same dependent variable as in the previous analyses. Secondly, we included variables measuring voters' evaluations of the

government and perceptions of the national economy (see Appendix A–C). The EU-level performance variables are less than ideal, however, because they do not measure parties' performance at the EU level. We used one indicator of whether voters view the EU as beneficial; and another indicator measures whether they feel represented by the EU. These indicators lack a clear attribution of responsibility to parties — but they do measure the perceived performance of the EU. The model also includes several control variables, including left–right ideology, strength of partisanship, age, education and gender.

Table 2 shows the results for the four predictors that measure the transfer hypothesis (governmental performance and evaluations of the economy) and *suis generis* hypothesis (perceptions of a democracy deficit and European identity). The reference group is, as in the previous analyses, voters who support government parties at both levels. As a test of East–West differences, we also included an interaction term between a predictor listed in the leftmost column and an East–West dummy variable. The interaction terms were added separately for each equation. For example, we first estimated a model that included an interaction term between governmental performance evaluations and the East–West dummy. On the basis of these results, we then computed the conditional coefficients listed in the table for the East and the West. We also indicate whether an interaction term is significant. Then, we

Table 2.   Predicting support for government parties across national/EP elections in Eastern and Western Europe

	Electoral choice					
	Defections to opposition parties in EP elections		Defections to government parties in EP elections		Support for opposition parties across elections	
	Interaction		Interaction		Interaction	
	East	West	East	West	East	West
	(Significant)		(Significant)		(Significant)	
Government performance	−0.92**	−1.9*	−1.0**	−2.0**	−1.6**	−3.2**
evaluations	(No)		(Yes)		(No)	
Economic perceptions	−0.02	−0.42**	−0.19**	−0.38**	−0.21	−0.03
	(No)		(Yes)		(No)	
EU represents citizens	−0.09	−0.07*	0.07	0.19**	−0.11	0.03
	(No)		(No)		(No)	
Integration support	−0.50**	0.10	−0.78**	−0.31**	−0.46**	−0.03
	(Yes)		(Yes)		(Yes)	

Entries are conditional coefficients from a multi-nominal logit analysis. Government supporters at national and EU elections are the reference category. *n*=9,025.
*, ** significance at the 0.05 and 0.01 level, respectively. European weight is used.
Source: 2004 European Election Survey.

estimated another model, this time including an interaction term between evaluations of the national economy and the East–West dummy. And so on.

The results underscore much of the previous analyses. First, national performance perceptions are very important in the West — but also in the East. Secondly, there is some evidence, again, for the *suis generis* hypothesis: perceptions of the democracy deficit affect vote choice in the predictable direction. For instance, when citizens believe the EU represents them, they are more likely to fall into the national opposition/EU government category. In other words, perceived positive democratic performance by the EU helps national governmental parties to boost their support in EU elections, just as the *suis generis* hypothesis predicts.

As far as East–West differences are concerned, they are mostly *insignificant*, except for the European identity predictor. For nearly all coefficients, the sign is in the same direction and the differences are insignificant. Note also that most coefficients have the same sign but tend to be larger in the West. These preliminary analyses therefore do not suggest that national and EU elections are viewed fundamentally differently across the former East–West divide. Instead, they seem to suggest that the magnitude tends to be larger in the West, presumably because voters had more time to connect performance evaluations to parties' status as a government or opposition party. In short, we see differences of degree but not a fundamentally different character. And we find evidence, again, for both the transfer and *suis generis* mechanisms.

Political Representation and System Satisfaction

We would like to push the analyses one step further. To this end, consider that the *suis generis* hypothesis assumes that voters actually distinguish fairly clearly between the national and EU levels. In contrast, the transfer hypothesis assumes that voters generalize from the national to the supranational level, thus distinguishing less clearly between the two levels. A different way to examine the plausibility of the transfer and the *suis generis* hypotheses is to examine the degree to which voters clearly discriminate between two institutional layers. For this purpose, the indicators from the two election studies are less-than-ideal, for two reasons. First, while they measure the performance of national conditions reasonably well, they are quite imperfect for the EU level. Secondly, the fact that parties are prominent at both levels means that voters inevitably pay considerable attention to the national level, even when they evaluate the EU. Is there evidence that allows us to examine how voters actually perceive the process of representation, independent of political parties?

Fortunately, Eurobarometer 52.0, conducted in 1999, contains several useful indicators that we use here to tease out a bit further whether citizens clearly discriminate between the two levels, as the *suis generis* hypothesis suggests. We particularly look to the question:

> Many important decisions are made by the European Union. They might be in the interest of people like yourself, or they might not. To

what extent do you feel you can rely on each of the following bodies to make sure that these decisions are in the interest of people like yourself?

Respondents also evaluated a series of institutions, including their national parliament, their national government, the European Commission and the European Parliament on a ten-point scale. Another set of questions asks whether citizens are satisfied with the way democracy works at the national and EU level, again asked in the same question.

The *suis generis* hypothesis would predict that citizens clearly distinguish between the two levels. Therefore, support for this hypothesis would emerge if perceptions of the quality of national representation predict satisfaction with national democracies; if EU representation perceptions predict satisfaction with EU democracy; and, finally, if representation perceptions from one level do *not* predict satisfaction with democracy at the other level. This would be the clearest signs that citizens attribute representational responsibilities separately to each level. In contrast, the transfer hypothesis would predict that national performance perceptions affect satisfaction with the national *and* EU democracy because the performance of the two institutional layers are hypothesized to be linked in voters' minds.

Table 3 shows the surprisingly clear results in support of the *suis generis* hypothesis. Representational perceptions at each level predict satisfaction with democracies at each level. And representational perceptions at the national (EU) level do not influence evaluations of democracies at the EU (national) level. Note that these results emerge despite the fact that the question wording might easily have produced cross-level consistency because the representational indicators were asked in the same question as the satisfaction with democracy indicators. This provides strong support for the *suis generis* hypothesis because it shows, for West European voters at least, that they systematically distinguish between the representational mechanisms at the two levels.

Conclusion

The nature of multi-level governance in the EU creates unique problems for understanding public behaviour in that the same political actors — national political parties — serve as the instruments of public accountability at both the national and EU levels. It thus becomes very difficult to disentangle the national-level and EU-level motivations of voters across different elections. While the literature on second-order elections has clearly demonstrated that national considerations influence, if not dominate, the behaviour of voters in EP election, it has been less obvious when and how EU considerations might impact voting behaviour across elections. We have thus sought to assess how both national and EU considerations might influence behaviour in the EU.

There is considerable evidence that voters generalize the national performance to the EU level. There is also quite a bit of support for the idea that citizens distinguish between the transfer and *suis generis* mechanisms. The aggregate approach tends to be biased in favour of the transfer hypothesis to

Table 3.   Relationship between perceptions of representational responsibility and
perceptions of democracy at the national and EU levels

Predictor	EU democracy	National democracy
National institutions represent citizens	−0.008	−0.099**
	(0.005)	(0.009)
EU institutions represent citizens	−0.08**	0.006
	(0.007)	(0.007)
Party preference	0.02	−0.12*
	(0.04)	(0.04)
Nation benefits	−0.24**	−0.14**
	(0.02)	(0.01)
Knowledge about EU	0.06**	0.004
	(0.01)	(0.01)
National economy positive	−0.07**	−0.12**
	(0.01)	(0.01)
Personal economy positive	−0.02	−0.02
	(0.01)	(0.01)
Age cohort: Young	−0.15**	−0.05
	(0.03)	(0.04)
Age cohort: Middle	−0.08*	−0.003
	(0.03)	(0.04)
Education	0.02**	0.002
	(0.003)	(0.005)
Left ideology	0.05	0.07
	(0.05)	(0.04)
Centrist ideology	−0.01	−0.01
	(0.01)	(0.01)
Income	−0.01	−0.04**
	(0.009)	(0.01)
Number of observations	14,023	14,035

Source: Eurobarometer (1999).

the detriment of the *suis generis* mechanism. Both perspectives, however, are
needed to explain more fully the complex nature of vote choices in multi-
level systems of governance.

We have not only found that EU considerations do indeed influence the
public, but also some clues as to the conditions that impact the relative
weight of national and EU considerations. Our analysis indicates that the
transfer hypothesis may be supported, in part, by the way in which EP elections are conducted. Voters appear to weigh EU concerns more heavily when
they are not focused on the performance of national political parties, for
example, in the context of political representation. However, national parties
establish the procedures governing EP elections, select the candidates for EP
office and control the content of EP campaigns. The current system of EP
elections thus inevitably links national issues, political parties and EU issues.
If European actors were allowed more control over EP elections, then these

mechanisms might begin to focus more on EU issues and we might observe a shift in the relative weight of the different concerns motivating voting behaviour in these elections. Additionally, it appears that government parties benefit more if voters positively assess parties' performance at the EU level.

All told, these patterns suggest that perceptions of multi-level institutions mediate the relative emphasis that voters place on national and EU issues. In other words, national issues may dominate EU issues in EP elections due to the relative weaknesses of the European Parliament and/or the perception of EP elections as disingenuous instruments of accountability. Additionally, voters may believe that governing parties are better positioned to influence EU issues and may thus be more inclined to look to EU issues in deciding to punish or reward these parties. In short, the way EU elections are organized increases the salience of national factors at the EU level. Future research efforts should then seek to better identify those variables that may mediate the salience of EU issues on voting behaviour across elections, and to identify the conditions under which the EU is evaluated *suis generis*.

Acknowledgement

The authors would like to thank Hermann Schmitt and the participants at the 2007 EES conference in Cadenabbia for their helpful comments; Rohrschneider also would like to thank the Netherlands Institute for Advanced Studies (NIAS), where he was a fellow during the 2008–2009 academic year, for its generous support during the final writing stages of this project.

Notes

1. We stipulate this condition because we view the decision to participate in an EU election as distinct from the choice of parties once a voter decides to cast a ballot.
2. Unfortunately, Carrubba and Timbone do not use individual-level performance evaluations. Consequently, their analysis does not directly examine the motives of voter — which is our primary objective.
3. The correlation coefficient between governmental performance and parties' EU performance is significant ($r=0.36$) though far from perfect. This suggests that the two performance dimensions are partially independent.
4. Given the lack of appropriate variables, we cannot sort out exactly why EU supporters are more likely to switch towards governmental parties than opponents of integration.

References

Anderson, Christopher J. 1998. When in doubt use proxies. Attitudes toward domestic politics and support for European integration. *Comparative Political Studies* 31, no. 5: 569–601.

Andeweg, Rudy. 1995. The reshaping of national party systems. *West European Politics* 18, no. 3: 58–78.

Caramani, Daniele. 2006. Is there a European electorate and what does it look like? Evidence from electoral volatility measures, 1976–2004. *West European Politics* 29, no. 1: 1–27.

Carrubba, Cliff, and Richard J. Timpone. 2005. Explaining vote switching across first- and second-order elections. *Comparative Political Studies* 38, no. 3: 260–81.

Dalton, Russell J. 2005. *Citizen politics: Public opinion and political parties in advanced industrial democracies.* Washington, DC: Congressional Quarterly Press.

Gabel, Matthew. 2000. European integration, voters and national politics. *West European Politics* 23, no. 4: 52–72.

Hix, Simon, and Michael Marsh. 2007. Punishment or protest?. *Journal of Politics* 69, no. 2: 495–510.

Hooghe, L., and G. Marks. 2008. A postfunctionalist theory of European integration: From permissive consensus to constraining dissensus. *British Journal of Political Science* 39: 1–23.

Koepke, Jason R., and Nils Ringe. 2006. The second-order election model in an enlarged Europe. *European Union Politics* 7, no. 3: 321–46.

Majone, Giandomenico. 1998. Europe's 'democratic deficit': The question of standards. *European Law Journal* 4, no. 1: 5–28.

Marks, Gary, Liesbet Hooghe, Moira Nelso, and Erica Edwards. 2006. Party competition and European integration in East and West: Different structure, same causality. *Comparative Political Studies* 39, no. 2: 155–75.

Marsh, Michael. 1998. Testing the second-order election model after four European elections. *British Journal of Political Science* 28: 591–607.

Reif, Karlheinz, and Hermann Schmitt. 1980. Nine 2nd-order national elections — A conceptual framework for the analysis of European election results. *European Journal of Political Research* 8, no. 1: 3–44.

Rohrschneider, Robert. 2002. The democracy deficit and mass support for an EU-wide government. *American Journal of Political Science* 46, no. 2: 463–75.

Rohrschneider, Robert, and Stephen Whitefield. 2007. Representation in new democracies: Party stances on European integration in post-communist Eastern Europe. *Journal of Politics* 69, no. 4: 1133–46.

Schmitt, Hermann. 2005. The European Parliament elections of June 2004: Still second-order?. *West European Politics* 28, no. 3: 650–79.

Schmitt, Hermann, Alberto Sanz, and Daniela Braun. 2008. Micro-foundations of second-order election theory: A theoretical reconstruction and empirical test. Staff Seminar at CEVIPOF, Paris.

Schmitt, Hermann, and Jacques Thomassen. 1999. *Political representation and legitimacy in the European Union.* Oxford: Oxford Univ. Press.

Tavits, Margit. 2005. The development of stable party support. Electoral dynamics in post-communist Europe. *American Journal of Political Science* 49, no. 2: 283–95.

Van der Brug, Wouter, Cees van der Eijk, and Mark Franklin. 2007. *The economy and the vote: Economic conditions in fifteen countries.* New York: Cambridge Univ. Press.

Appendix A: Measurement of Government Support — EES (1999)

Dependent Variables

- *Government support across national/EP elections*: We coded respondents as (1) voted for a party in a governing coalition in the last EP election and the last general election, (2) voted for a party in a governing coalition in the last EP election and a party not in a governing coalition in the last general election, (3) voted for a party not in a governing coalition in the last EP election and a party in a governing coalition in the last general election and (4) voted for a party not in a governing coalition in the last EP election and the last general election.

Independent Variables

- *Parties' EU performance*: 'Thinking once again about European integration, how satisfied or dissatisfied are you with the current policy in <name of your country>? Are you (1) very satisfied, (2) somewhat satisfied, (4) somewhat dissatisfied or (5) very dissatisfied?' We included the small number of don't know responses as a (3) middle category.
- *Parties' government performance*: 'Let us now come back to <name of your country>. Do you (1) approve or (3) disapprove of the government's record to date?' We included the small number of don't know responses as a (3) middle category.
- *Economic perceptions*: 'How about the state of the economy, how satisfied or dissatisfied are you with the current policy in <name of your country>: are you (1) very satisfied, (2) somewhat satisfied, (4) somewhat dissatisfied or (5) very dissatisfied?' We included the small number of don't know responses as a (3) middle category.
- *EU support*: 'Generally speaking, do you think that <your country's > membership of the European Union is (1) a bad thing, (2) neither a good nor a bad thing or (3) a good thing?' We placed the small number of don't know responses in the (2) category.
- *Party identification*: We created a dichotomous variable: (1) if the respondent identified themselves as 'very close to <their party of choice>, fairly close, or merely a sympathizer' and (0) if they did not identify with a party or gave did not know.
- *Far-left ideology*: Taking the respondent's self-placement on a ten-point ideology scale (1–10), we classified them as (1) far-left if they answered 1–3 and (0) for any other answer.
- *Left-centre ideology*: Taking the respondent's self-placement on a ten-point ideology scale (1–10), we classified them as (1) left of centre if they answered 4 and (0) for any other answer.
- *Right-centre ideology*: Taking the respondent's self-placement on a ten-point ideology scale (1–10), we classified them as (1) right of centre if they answered 6 and (0) for any other answer.
- *Right ideology*: Taking the respondent's self-placement on a ten-point ideology scale (1–10), we classified them as (1) right if they answered 7 and (0) for any other answer.
- *Far-right ideology*: Taking the respondent's self-placement on a ten-point ideology scale (1–10), we classified them as (1) far-right if they answered 8–10 and (0) for any other answer.
- *Age*: 'What year were you born?'
- *Education*: 'How old were you when you stopped full-time education?'
- *Sex*: (0) male, (1) female

Appendix B: Measurement of Government Support — EES (2004)

Dependent Variables

Government support across national/EP elections: We coded respondents as (1) voted for a party in a governing coalition in the last EP election and the last general election, (2) voted for a party in a governing coalition in the last EP election and a party not in a governing coalition in the last general election, (3) voted for a party not in a governing coalition in the last EP election and a party in a governing coalition in the last general election and (4) voted for a party not in a governing coalition in the last EP election and the last general election.

Independent Variables

- *EU represents citizens*: An additive index of two questions about the government's economic performance. 'How much confidence do you have that decisions made by the European Union will be in the interest of (1) [country] and (2) people like you?' The indicator ranges from (2) doesn't feel represented to (10) feels represented.
- *Support for integration*: 'Generally speaking, do you think that [country's] membership of the European Union is a good thing, a bad thing, or neither good nor bad?' (1) Bad thing, (2) Neither, Don't know, (3) Good thing.
- *Parties' government performance*: 'Let us now come back to [country]. Do you approve or disapprove the government's record to date?' Respondents could answer (0) disapprove or (2) approve. We included the small number of don't know responses as a (1) middle category.
- *Economic perceptions*: An additive index of two questions about the government's economic performance. 'What do you think about the economy? Compared to 12 months ago, do you think that the general economic situation in this country is a lot worse, a little worse, stayed the same, a little better or a lot better?' and 'Over the next 12 months, how do you think the general economic situation in this country will: get a lot worse, get a little worse, stay the same, get a little better or get a lot better?' The indicator ranges from (2) bad performance to (10) good performance.

Appendix C: Measurement of Representation Variables — Eurobarometer 52.0 (1999)

Dependent Variables

- *Satisfaction with EU democracy*: 'On the whole are you (1) very satisfied, (2) fairly satisfied, (4) not very satisfied or (5) not at all satisfied with the way democracy works in the European Union?' We included the small number of don't know responses as a (4) middle category.
- *Satisfaction with national democracy*: 'On the whole are you (1) very satisfied, (2) fairly satisfied, (4) not very satisfied or (5) not at all satisfied with the way democracy works in <our country>?' We included the small number of don't know responses as a (4) middle category.

Independent Variables

- *National institutions and EU institutions represent citizens*: 'Many important decisions are made by the European Union. They might be in the interest of people like yourself, or they might not. To what extent do you feel you can rely on each of the following bodies to make sure that these decisions are in the interest of people like yourself?' Respondents placed the national government, national parliament, European Commission and European Parliament on a ten-point scale, ranging from (1) cannot rely on it at all to (10) can rely on it completely.
- *Party preference*: Respondent would support a party in government if there was an election next Sunday (coded 1) or an opposition party (coded 0).
- *Nation benefits*: 'Taking everything into consideration, would you say that <our country> has on balance benefited or not from being a member of the European Union?' We included the small number of don't know responses as a middle category.
- *Knowledge about EU*: A four-point indicator (0–4) based on the number of correct answers to four factual questions about the (i) President of the EU Commission; (ii) a European commissioner appointed by national government; (iii) (National) Minister of Finance; (iv) National Minister of Foreign Affairs.
- *National economy positive*: An additive index of two questions about the future economic situation. 'What are your expectations for the year to come: will 2000 be better, worse, or the same, when it comes to: (1) the economic situation in <our country>; (2) the employment situation in <our country>?' The indicator ranges from 2 (worse) to 6.
- *Personal economy positive*: Same question lead as for national economy, after which respondents evaluated: (1) the financial situation of your household; (2) your personal job situation. The indicator ranges from 2 (worse) to 6.
- *Age cohort: Young*: Dichotomous variable: (1) respondents aged 15–29; (0) respondents all other ages.
- *Age cohort: Middle*: Dichotomous variable: (1) respondents aged 30–50; (0) respondents all other ages.
- *Education*: Years of schooling. Respondents 'still studying' were coded to the mean year of schooling for that nation.
- *Left ideology*: Taking the respondent's self-placement on a ten-point ideology scale (1–10), we classified them as (1) left if they answered 1–3 and (0) for any other answer.
- *Centrist ideology*: Taking the respondent's self-placement on a ten-point ideology scale (1–10), we classified them as (1) centre if they answered 4–6 and (0) for any other answer.
- *Income*: Four-point indicator ranging from low to high, with missing data recoded to the mean income for that country.

The Clarity of Policy Alternatives, Left–Right and the European Parliament Vote in 2004

ANDRÉ FREIRE*, MARINA COSTA LOBO** &
PEDRO MAGALHÃES**

*ISCTE — Lisbon University Institute, Lisbon, Portugal **ICS-UL, Social Sciences Research Institute, University of Lisbon, Lisbon, Portugal

ABSTRACT The importance of the left–right divide for party choice is well established, both for legislative and European Parliament (EP) elections. However, the conditions under which left–right self-placement becomes more or less important in explaining the vote in both legislative and EP elections are clearly understudied. The article uses the 2004 EP elections as a laboratory to understand if there are indeed systematic differences between political systems' characteristics that might explain variation in terms of the strength of the relationship between left–right self-placement and the vote. Using the survey data from the European Election Study 2004 (twenty-one EU member states), the paper has two goals. First, to examine whether citizens' left–right self-placement has a different impact on the vote in different types of democratic regime, defined in terms of the contrast between consolidating and long-established democracies. Secondly, to examine whether this contrast resists the introduction of controls for three other factors hypothesized to make a difference in the extent to which left–right orientations have a greater influence on the vote: the permissiveness of electoral system; the clarity of policy alternatives provided by the party system; and the particular type of party alignments along both the left–right and anti-/pro-integration scales that tend to characterize each country. Our findings corroborate that (the 2004 EP) elections do seem to be about choosing parties in terms of left–right orientations to a considerable extent. Furthermore, we found that the usefulness of left–right orientations as cues to the vote seems to be contingent upon a major contextual factor: greater levels of clarity of the policy alternatives provided by the party system render citizens' left–right self-placement more consequential for their EP vote. Finally, we found that left–right orientations may not be equally useful in consolidating and in the remaining established democracies.

Correspondence Address: André Freire, ISCTE — Lisbon University Institute, Lisbon, Portugal. E-mail: andre.freire@iscte.pt

The Importance and Meaning of the Left–Right Divide in Mass Politics

The meaning and importance (namely in explaining the vote) of the left–right divide is well established (Inglehart and Klingemann 1976, 245; Huber 1989; Knutsen 1995, 1997; Freire 2006a, 2006b, 2008b). Interestingly, European Parliament elections do not seem to be particularly different in this respect. As 'second-order' elections, European elections tend to be dominated by considerations pertaining to the national political arena, where the role of left–right orientations is predominant. Thus, several studies have shown the importance of the left–right divide to explain voting choices in EP elections (Van der Eijk, Franklin, and Oppenhuis 1996; Van der Brug and Van der Eijk 1999; Van der Eijk, Franklin, and Van der Brug 1999; Van der Brug and Franklin 2005). Studies on electoral behaviour in legislative elections have shown that individuals' left–right self-placement is a major predictor of their voting choices and that, in fact, its importance has been increasing in many countries over recent decades (Franklin, Mackie, and Valen 1992; Gunther and Montero 2001).

However, the contextual conditions under which the left–right cleavage can become more or less important in explaining the vote in European elections remain somewhat understudied. This paper seeks to determine under what conditions the left–right divide is more or less important in explaining the vote in EP elections. We use European elections as a 'laboratory' to understand electoral behaviour in general, precisely because these electoral contests take place simultaneously under different social, political and institutional conditions. Thus, using the survey data from the European Election Study 2004,[1] the present paper has two major goals.

The first goal is to examine whether the ideological location of citizens — in terms of left–right self-placement — has a different impact on the vote in different types of democratic regime. Several studies have suggested that the most consequential difference in this respect is the one between the former communist democracies and the Western established democracies in the EU. However, we will examine whether this particular difference is indeed consequential and, above all, if it resists the introduction of several other variables not considered in previous research. Two of those variables are readily familiar. First, as research on national elections already suggests, countries whose electoral system is less permissive — i.e. with greater barriers to representation of smaller parties — tend to exhibit a lower influence of left–right self-placement on the vote, by giving incentives to parties and party leaders to adopt centrist and catch-all strategies and appeals. We wish to examine whether this is also true in the case of EP elections.

Secondly, since this relationship between institutional features of the electoral system and the ideological distinctiveness and clarity of partisan alternatives is only a probabilistic one, we will also test the hypothesis that the actual (perceived) clarity of policy alternatives available to citizens also makes a difference in the extent to which voters resort to the left–right heuristics in order to make voting choices.

Finally, we will test the hypothesis that the particular type of party alignments along both the left–right and anti-/pro-integration scales that tend to characterize each country also affect the extent to which ideological orientations affect the vote. More specifically, we will test whether left–right orientations become a more consequential explanation of the vote in EP elections when competition within the party system is based on reinforcing or congruent alignments in terms of both left–right and anti-/pro-integration stances on the part of political parties.

In the following (second) section, we specify our hypotheses (and the rationale behind each of them), the data used and the methods employed. Then, in the third section, we describe the distribution of the independent variables in the twenty-one countries/political systems on which data are available. In the fourth section, our hypotheses are tested against empirical data. In the final section, we present some concluding remarks.

Hypotheses, Data and Methods

Our initial hypothesis (H1) is that *the impact of left–right orientations on voting choices in EP elections should be lower in the former communist countries*. These democracies, which we will henceforth designate as 'consolidating democracies', have been seen as particularly distinctive from others given the suppression of class and religious differences, the totalitarian or post-totalitarian nature of previous regimes, and the social structural conditions inherited from the communist past. These have arguably contributed to a 'flattening' of the social landscape, with the consequence of weakening political and ideological attachments and rendering the left–right schema less useful for voters (White, Rose, and McAllister 1997; Lawson, Rommele, and Karasimeonov 1999). Furthermore, as more recent democracies, they are less likely to exhibit high levels of party system institutionalization — stable and legitimized organizations, regular patterns of party competition, and the existence of relatively strong attachments to existing parties on the part of voters. Where these elements are absent, party ideological placements and electoral choices tend to exhibit high levels of instability and fluidity (Mainwaring 1999; Mainwaring and Torcal 2005). This general hypothesis has found confirmation in the work of Van der Brug and Franklin (2005). However, they have also shown that this difference between the consolidating and the remaining democracies is significantly reduced when other contextual factors are taken into account. Thus, our first goal is to examine if this difference between the EU member states is indeed consequential in and of its own and, above all, if it resists the introduction of several other contextual factors not considered in previous research.

What other factors are those? They concern electoral institutions and the way party competition is structured along the left–right and anti-/pro-EU integration dimensions in European countries. Since the work of Anthony Downs (1957, 114–41), two-party systems are usually associated with a unimodal distribution of voters' preferences over the left–right continuum, with most of the voters concentrated in the central positions of this political divide, and with political parties competing mainly for the median (centrist) voter. Thus, in two-party systems there is a drive towards ideological moderation. On the contrary, multi-party systems are usually associated with multimodal distributions of voters' preferences over the left–right continuum. Moreover, the different parties have more incentives to concentrate their appeals in specific segments of the electorate (socially, politically and ideologically defined). Thus, in the latter systems there is usually a drive towards ideological polarization, and sometimes even to centrifugal competition (see Sani and Sartori 1983; Sartori 1992). In addition, it is well established in the literature about electoral and party systems that there is a strong association between the level of proportionality of the electoral system and the degree of fragmentation of the party system (see, for example, Lijphart 1994). And, even more to the point, Norris (2004) has shown that electoral behaviour in systems with higher thresholds seems to be less determined by cleavage politics, including left–right ideology, given the incentives of parties in those systems to adopt cross-cutting and catch-all appeals.

Therefore, bearing in mind these theoretical contributions, we will start by focusing on whether the more or less permissive character of the European Parliament electoral system (measured through the effective threshold) influences the extent to which the left–right divide is related to vote choices. More specifically, our second hypothesis (H2) states that *the higher the permissiveness of the electoral system, the higher the impact of the left–right orientations on the vote* (unless stated otherwise, we are always referring to the vote in EP elections). It might be argued that, although this is indeed expected, there are other plausible possibilities. Namely, that (especially in European elections) the more permissive an electoral system, the higher the probability that it allows the entrance of new parties that do not compete (at least mainly) on the left–right axis. We acknowledge that is a real possibility. However, we also believe that it is mainly an empirical question for us to determine whether a more permissive electoral system indeed increases (or depresses) the importance of left–right self-placement on the vote.

However, we need to take into account the fact that the relationship between the electoral system and the extent to which the party system provides clear and distinct policy alternatives is merely probabilistic. To put it another way, we can find fragmented party systems both with high and with low levels of ideological polarization — remember Sartori's (1992) definition of 'segmented pluralism' and 'polarized pluralism' — because the permissiveness of the electoral system (or the party system format) only establish conditions more or less propitious to the clarity of policy alternatives as they present themselves in the left–right spectrum. Consequently, we also need more direct measures of the construct 'clarity of policy alternatives'.

One possible approach is to test if *party system polarization* influences the extent to which left–right self-placement influences the vote. Several studies have documented the importance of ideological polarization at the systemic level to explain citizens' political attitudes and behaviour (Nie and

Andersen 1974; Bartolini and Mair 1990, 193–211, 251–85; Knutsen and Kumlin 2005; Berglund et al. 2005; Van der Eijk, Schmitt, and Binder 2005; Freire 2006a, 2008b). However, none of these studies used party system ideological polarization to explain the differential impact of left–right self-placement on the vote (in European or legislative elections) or, if they did, it was for a very small set of countries (Van der Eijk, Schmitt, and Binder 2005).[2] Our hypothesis (H3a) is that *the more polarized are the policy alternatives presented by the parties to the voters, the more easily can they differentiate between parties on the left–right spectrum and, thus, left–right self-placement will be more consequential for vote choices.* In such situations, voters will be more prone to think about left and right in terms of issues and to relate the left–right divide with social cleavages. In those conditions, it will be easier for citizens to use the left–right as a short-cut to cope with the complexities of the political universe, and to decide which parties to vote for.

Finally, we want to test the hypothesis that the relevance of citizens' left–right self-placement to predict EP vote should be contingent upon the particular structure of political contestation in each country, particularly upon the way parties are positioned along the left–right and anti-/pro-EU integration political divides. There are four models of political conflict in the European Union (Steenbergen and Marks 2004). The 'international relations model' predicts that conflict in the European Union is structured around a single dimension: a continuum from 'less integration (defend national sovereignty)' to 'more integration (promote supranational governance' (*ibid.*, 5–6). According to this model there is no relation between this conflict-axis and the historical left–right divide. The 'regulation model' (Tsebelis and Garret 2000) also predicts a single dimension of conflict over European integration; however, it is completely subsumed under the left–right divide: the continuum goes from 'left/high regulation at the EU level' to 'right/low regulation at the EU level', and the prominence of the left–right divide is explained by the second-order nature of EU politics vis-à-vis domestic politics. The other two models, the Hix–Lord model (Hix and Lord 1997; Hix 1999, 2005) and the Hooghe–Marks model (Hooghe and Marks 1999), predict two dimensions of conflict over European integration. However, while the Hix–Lord model predicts two orthogonal dimensions of competition (left vs. right and more vs. less integration), the Hooghe–Marks model predicts that the two dimensions (left vs. right and more vs. less integration) are neither completely orthogonal, nor fused. From the partial overlapping of these two dimensions results an opposition between 'regulated capitalism' (on the left and more integration quadrant) vs. 'neoliberalism' (on the right and less integration quadrant).

The evidence that resulted from testing these four models is rather mixed (Marks 2004), but the major lesson is perhaps that the overlapping (or cross-cutting) between the two dimensions of conflict varies across countries, issues, arenas and actors (Marks 2004; see also Taggart 1998; Hooghe, Marks, and Wilson 2004; Brinegar, Jolly, and Kitschelt 2004; Gabel and Hix 2004; Ray 2004; Taggart and Szczerbiak 2004; Bartolini 2005). Our hypothesis is that such variation affects the extent to which left–right self-placements are consequential for voting decisions in EP elections. More specifically, we know that the usefulness of the left–right scale for voters tends to increase when the nature of party competition within the party system involves a uni-dimensional alignment or reinforcing alignments (Kitschelt et al. 1999). Thus, according to our fourth hypothesis (H4), *in those countries where political parties' orientations towards European integration represents a political divide that is encapsulated by the left–right cleavage (i.e. where both dimensions of competition are congruent), citizens' left–right self-placement should also be a more relevant predictor of EP vote.* The reverse should be true for those countries where the two dimensions of competition are not congruent.

The independent variables mentioned above are all contextual variables measured at the macro-level, whose effects on the vote, in cross-level interaction with left–right self-placement, we wish to determine. However, we also employ some independent variables measured at the individual-level, namely: gender; age (a recoding of year of birth); education (age when respondent ended full-time education);[3] subjective social class (a five-point scale ranging from working to upper class); religiosity (a recoding of the mass attendance variable); and unionization (a dichotomous variable with '0' not a member of a union and '1' self- or someone in the family is a member). The European Election Study (EES) 2004 integrated database will be used in this paper. However, for several reasons it was not possible to include all twenty-five member states in the study. First, it was not possible to field a survey in Malta. Also, Belgium, Lithuania and Sweden were removed from the database since their studies did not ask respondents certain key questions that are fundamental for our paper, namely q14_x and/or q22_x, i.e. those questions that ask respondents to place each party on a left–right scale, and on a pro- and anti- more European integration scale. Northern Ireland was also excluded. Thus, the list of country cases included in our analysis are the following: Austria, Britain, Cyprus, Czech Republic, Denmark, Estonia, Finland, France, Germany, Greece, Hungary, Ireland, Italy, Latvia, Luxembourg, The Netherlands, Poland, Portugal, Slovakia, Slovenia and Spain.

Institutional and Political Conditions for the Impact of the Left–Right Divide in Each Polity

Table 1 presents the main characteristics of the electoral systems used in the countries being analysed. All of the member states use proportional electoral systems for the EP elections, even though formulae vary. The overwhelming majority of countries have single electoral districts, and average district magnitude is 24.8. Concerning the effective threshold, which is the contextual variable being used in the model below, it was computed as 75 per cent/(Mean District Magnitude + 1).[4] The lower the effective threshold the more permissive in relation to the representation of smaller parties it is. Table 1 shows that, considering only the average values, there are no significant differences between post-communist countries and the others

Table 1.   The electoral systems for EP elections

Country	Electoral formula	No MEPs	No of districts	Mean M	Effective threshold
Austria	Hare/d'Hondt	18	1	18	4.0
Britain	d'Hondt	75	11	6.8	9.6
Cyprus	PR.(n.a.)	6	1	6	10.7
Denmark	d'Hondt	14	1	14	5.0
Finland	d'Hondt	14	1	14	5.0
France	d'Hondt	78	8	9.8	6.9
Germany	Hare-Niemayer	99	1	99	5.0
Greece	Hagen-Bischoff	24	1	24	3.0
Ireland	STV	13	4	3.3	17.4
Italy	Hare	78	1	78	4.1[a]
Luxembourg	Hagen-Bischoff	6	1	6	10.7
The Netherlands	Hare/d'Hondt	27	1	27	2.7
Portugal	d'Hondt	24	1	24	3.0
Spain	d'Hondt	54	1	54	1.4
Average	—	37.9	2.4	27.4	6.5
Czech Rep.	d'Hondt	24	1	24	3.0
Estonia	d'Hondt	6	1	6	10.7
Hungary	d'Hondt	24	1	24	5.0
Latvia	Sainte-Lague	9	1	9	7.5
Poland	d'Hondt	54	1	54	5.0
Slovakia	Hagen-Bischoff	14	1	14	5.0
Slovenia	d'Hondt	7	1	7	9.4
Average	—	19.7	1.0	19.7	6.5

[a]In the Italian case, we follow Farrell and Scully (2005) and take into account the allocation of seats on the basis of rankings on regional lists.
Source: European Parliament, authors' own calculations.

concerning this measure: the average thresholds for both sets of countries is 6.5 per cent.

Table 2 presents indicators used to capture the extent to which voters perceive the policy positions of parties clearly and distinctively. As we can see in Table 2, two alternative measures of party system polarization were computed. First, using voters' perceptions of parties' location on the left–right scale (left, 1; right, 10), we started by computing the ideological distance between the interpolated median[5,6] of the two major parties (usually, these parties are one from the left, the other from the right; the only exceptions are Ireland, Latvia, Estonia and Poland) in each polity. Secondly, using again voters' perceptions of parties' location in the left–right scale (left, 1; right, 10), we started by computing the ideological distance between the interpolated median positions in the left–right scale of the two extreme parties (one from the left, other from the right) with electoral representation in the European Parliament.[7]

Table 2. Party systems' left–right polarization (two alternative measures)

Countries	Difference median (IM) two major parties	Difference median (IM) two most extreme parties
Austria	2.64	4.62
Britain	1.91	2.14
Denmark	3.00	6.42
Finland	2.17	6.57
France	3.92	8.14
Germany	2.91	5.77
Greece	2.77	7.28
Ireland	0.27	3.97
Italy	5.72	8.00
Luxembourg	2.76	2.76
The Netherlands	3.11	6.08
Portugal	2.96	5.70
Spain	4.96	6.32
Cyprus	7.66	7.66
Average	3.34	5.82
Czech Republic	7.76	7.76
Estonia	0.78	3.06
Hungary	5.73	5.73
Latvia	0.59	5.97
Slovakia	4.47	5.06
Slovenia	4.24	4.28
Poland	0.84	6.44
Average post-communist	3.49	5.47

The indicators do not all point exactly in the same direction. The ideological distance is smaller in post-communist countries between parties on the extremes of the party system, but higher if we take the two largest parties. Besides, there is also a predictable correlation between the permissiveness of the electoral system and the extent to which the party system exhibits left–right integration polarization. The correlations, however, although they have the predicted signs (negative: higher threshold, less polarization) are of medium or high strength: -0.340 for the major parties (not significant at the 0.05 level); -0.538 for the extreme parties (not significant at the 0.05 level).

The final contextual element contained in our hypotheses is the extent to which left and right and anti- vs. pro-Europe party stances exhibit congruence, i.e. the extent to which both orientations form a uni-dimensional map of political competition or not (Table 3). Such congruence has been studied through the lens of voters' perceptions (van der Eijk and Franklin 2004), through Euromanifestos data (Gabel and Hix 2004), through expert surveys (Hooghe, Marks, and Wilson 2004; Steenbergen and Scott 2004) and Member of the European Parliament (MEP) behaviour (Thomassen, Noury,

Table 3.   Congruence between left–right and the European issue — correlation between respondent's median (IM) placement of each party on the left–right scale and the anti-/pro-European scale (absolute values)

Country	Congruence
Austria	0.59
Britain	0.47
Denmark	0.32
Finland	0.80
France	0.01
Germany	0.08
Greece	0.45
Ireland	0.94
Italy	0.35
Luxembourg	0.86
The Netherlands	0.59
Portugal	0.71
Spain	0.41
Cyprus	0.95
Average	0.54
Czech Republic	0.39
Estonia	0.91
Hungary	0.50
Latvia	0.99
Poland	0.52
Slovakia	0.96
Slovenia	0.90
Average post-communist	0.74
Average all countries	0.60

and Voeten 2004). We operationalized *congruence between the European integration issue and the left–right divide* in each country/political system in the following way. Using voters' perceptions of parties' location in the left–right scale and in the European integration scale[8] ('unification has already gone too far', 1; 'unification should be pushed further', 10), we mapped for each country and each of the parties represented in the EP the interpolated median positions in each one of the above-mentioned scales. In order to produce a summary measure of congruence, we simply computed the correlation of these interpolated median positions of all parties in each country, and used the absolute value of that correlation as an indicator of congruence. Thus, the exercise is identical to that performed by Van der Eijk and Franklin (2004, chapter 2). However, it is not redundant for at least two reasons. First, because the data used by the authors are from EES 1999, whereas we are using data from EES 2004. It is shown elsewhere that parties' positioning both on the left–right cleavage, and especially on the anti-/pro-integration stance has varied substantially over the years (Gabel and Hix 2004, 108–9). Secondly, because, for the first time, indicators on congruence are presented concerning seven post-communist countries and Cyprus.

Congruence between respondents' placement of parties on a left–right scale and on a pro-/anti-European scale *is substantially higher in the newer (post-communist) democracies*, independently of whether direction of the relationship is positive or negative. Also, the inverted U-curve is found less in these new members of the EU. Indeed, it is found only in the party placement of the Czech Republic, with all other post-communist countries exhibiting strong linear correlations, mostly positive.

Looking at all countries in Table 3, average congruence is 0.60. Comparing with Van der Eijk and Franklin's (2004) graphs, there seem to be no significant changes. In twelve countries, the correlation is positive, meaning that there is a tendency for right-wing parties to be viewed as more pro-integration than left-wing parties. This is especially true in Luxembourg, Ireland, Cyprus, Estonia, Slovakia, Slovenia and Latvia — cases where the correlations are particularly strong. In these countries, the correlation of the median (IM) perceptions of respondents concerning parties' positioning on the left–right scale and anti-/pro-European scale, is positive and equal to or higher than 0.86. In several other countries, where correlations are lower than in the cases mentioned above, we can identify an inverted U-curve (see Freire, Lobo, and Magalhães 2007, Annex 1). This is evident in the Czech Republic, Denmark, Greece, Portugal and the Netherlands. And, in three countries, there is no discernable relationship between positioning of political parties on the left–right scale and on the anti-/pro-European scale: France, Italy and Germany. There are therefore three different patterns: an inverted U-curve; linear relationships or an orthogonal relationship.

Testing the Hypotheses

One crucial problem when testing the previous hypotheses using data from all these different European countries concerns how to conceive of the dependent variable. Different countries have different party systems, and it is impossible to achieve a common coding for all available options without imposing a particular structure to the vote choice that may or may not be the most relevant in each country. Thus, we adopted two alternative strategies of analysis: one in which such structure is imposed and one in which it is not.

First, we coded each valid vote for a party that elected at least one MEP as that party's location in the left–right axis, more specifically, with the value of the (interpolated) median perceptions of respondents concerning the ideological positioning of those parties (variables q14_1 to q14_4). We then used a multi-level linear regression analysis to estimate a model where party choice was regressed on a number of socio-demographic variables (gender, age, education, religiosity, social class and affiliation with a trade union) and each individual voter's position on the left–right scale.[9] We expect, obviously, left–right self-placement to play a relevant role in these choices, even after socio-demographic variables are taken into account. However, we test our hypotheses by estimating cross-level interaction effects, more specifically, interactions between individual left–right self-placement and the macro-level variables described in the previous section. The results are presented in Table 4. Models 1 and 2 present alternative specifications of the model, using the two different measures of party system polarization described above.

The results show, first, that all of the individual-level variables have the predictable effects. Members of trade unions are less likely to vote for parties placed to the right of the party system, while more religious individuals, of higher social classes and positioned ideologically more to the right all tend more to vote for parties on the right. Concerning our hypotheses, only one seems to hold: the greater the clarity of policy alternatives provided by the party system — measured either (as in model 2) as the ideological distance between the most extreme parties or (as in model 1) between the largest parties — the more consequential to vote choices seems individual ideological placements in the left–right scale (confirming H3).

However, in this analysis, we imposed a left–right dimensionality on the vote choice. To avoid this problem, we analysed the data in an alternative way. For each one of the twenty-one countries under analysis, we estimated two separated multinomial logistic regressions: first, only with the socio-demographic variables mentioned above; secondly, with those variables plus left–right self-placement. The dependent variable for each analysis was a

Table 4. Multi-level model of vote choices in EP elections (median left–right position per party as dependent variable)

	Model 1	Model 2
Intercept	5.72 (0.13)***	5.72 (0.13)***
Female	−0.12 (0.06)*	−0.13 (0.06)*
Age	0.003 (0.003)	0.002 (0.003)
Education	−0.004 (0.005)	−0.004 (0.006)
Social class	0.24 (0.05)***	0.27 (0.05)***
Trade Union	−0.34 (0.07)***	−0.38 (0.07)***
Religiosity	0.20 (0.04)***	0.22 (0.04)***
Left–right self-placement (LRSP)	0.16 (0.04)***	0.12 (0.05)*
LRSP*Post-Communist	0.03 (0.09)	0.06 (0.09)
LRSP*Threshold	−0.02 (0.01)	−0.01 (0.02)
LRSP*Polarization (larger parties)	0.07 (0.01)***	—
LRSP*Polarization (most extreme parties)	—	0.04 (0.01)**
LRSP*Congruence	−0.04 (0.12)	0.16 (0.16)
Level-2 variance component	0.40	0.40
Level-1 variance component	3.47	3.77
Level-2 cases	21	
Level-1 observations	10,530	

*p<0.05; **p<0.01; ***p<0.001; all countries equally weighted; level-1 variables centred around group-mean; level-2 variables centred around grand mean; robust standard errors in parentheses.

discrete, non-ordered variable: the party vote in the 2004 Euro Parliament elections, in each country, including all vote choices that were made by at least 3 per cent of each national sample (the minimum found that allowed a multinomial logistic analysis without empty cells). Next, we computed the difference in the variance explained (Nagelkerke) by the two regressions. This difference represents the contribution of ideology to the explanation of the vote after controlling for the socio-demographic variables, in each country. This difference was then turned into the dependent variable in a linear regression analysis: we test for the impact of all the contextual variables refereed above upon the size of left–right effects on the vote. In other words, as in the previous multi-level analysis, we want to determine which contextual factors mediate the impact of ideology in vote choices, but do it this time without imposing any dimensionality on vote choices. The results are presented in Table 5. Again, models 1 and 2 present two different specifications, using alternative measures of the polarization variable.

The results confirm those obtained with the full multi-level analysis: in countries where ideological polarization is largest, regardless of how we measure it, ideology matters more for vote choices (H3). The important thing, however, is to note that this is also the case when, unlike in the previous analysis, we do not impose a particular dimensionality on vote choices. The distance between the largest parties in the system is more consequential from this point of view — as already happened in the multi-level analysis — than the distance between the most extreme parties and, on the basis of the R^2 values, the fit of model 1 is much better than that of model 2. One way to make these results more vivid is to consider Figure 1, where the degree of party system polarization (as perceived by voters) between the two largest parties in the system is plotted against the predicted values of model 1. Clearly, in more polarized systems, left–right self-placement brings a greater contribution to explain vote choices (confirming H3).

Table 5. Macro-level correlates of the impact of left–right on vote choices in EP elections (increased pseudo-R^2 of left–right self-placement in each country as dependent variable)

	Model 1		Model 2	
	b (s.e.)	Beta	b (s.e.)	Beta
Constant	0.04 (0.09)		−0.20 (0.25)	
Post-communist	−0.16 (0.07)*	−0.39	−0.08 (0.09)	−0.19
Electoral threshold	−0.02 (0.01)	−0.30	−0.01 (0.01)	−0.18
Ideological polarization (largest parties)	0.08 (0.02)***	0.75	—	—
Ideological polarization (most extreme parties)	—	—	0.06 (0.03)*	0.57
Congruence in left–right and pro-/anti-Europe	0.04 (0.13)	0.06	0.24 (0.18)	0.36
n		21		21
R^2		0.62		0.33

*$p<0.05$; **$p<0.01$; ***$p<0.001$.

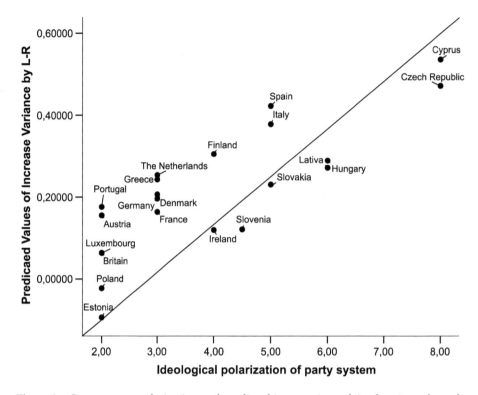

Figure 1. Party system polarization and predicted increase in explained variance brought about by ideological self-placement.

There is, however, an important difference between these results and those obtained with the multi-level model. The results from model 1 suggest that, as proposed by hypothesis 1 (H1), left–right is less consequential for the vote in consolidating democracies, particularly in model 1. This calls attention to two aspects. First, imposing a particular dimensionality to vote choices in the analysis is not indifferent to the results. Secondly, this means that, in one of our results, the specificity of the consolidating democracies in terms of the impact of ideology in vote choices does not disappear entirely, even when clarity of political alternatives is taken into account.

Concluding Remarks

As stated at the outset, the present paper had two major goals. First, to examine whether citizens' left–right self-placement has a different impact on the vote in different types of democratic regime, i.e. in terms of consolidating versus long-established democracies defined as post communist democracies versus all the rest. Secondly, to examine whether the generic differences found between democracies in terms of their level of democratic 'consolidation' or 'establishment' resist the introduction of controls for three other factors hypothesized to make a difference in the extent to which left–right orientations have a greater (or lesser) influence on the vote: the more or less permissive character of the electoral system; the clarity of policy alternatives presented by political parties to the electorate in each polity; and the congruence (or lack of congruence) between the left–right and the pro-/anti-European dimensions of party competition. We used European elections as a 'laboratory' to understand electoral behaviour in general, precisely because these electoral contests take place simultaneously under different social, political and institutional conditions. The survey data are from the European Election Study 2004: twenty-one member countries/political systems were analysed.

Our findings corroborate previous research in confirming that the 2004 EP elections do seem to be about choosing parties in terms of left–right orientations to a considerable extent. Furthermore, we found that the usefulness of left–right orientations as cues to the vote seems to be contingent upon a major contextual factor: the clarity of the policy alternatives provided by the party system. In this respect, the indicator that measures polarization between the two largest parties proved to have a greater explanatory power, but the indicator that measures polarization between the parties at the extremes of the party system also points in the same direction. The differences concern solely the relative strength of the relationships. Both of these findings are congruent with previous work on different types of elections, focusing on the contextual factors that mediate the impact of values on party choice (Knutsen and Kumlin 2005) or on social and partisan identities on left–right self-placement (Freire 2008b).

Finally, we found that left–right orientations may not be equally useful in consolidating and in the remaining established democracies. In the multi-level analysis where we imposed a left–right dimensionality on vote choices, no significant differences remain between former communist countries and the remaining member states. However, when our dependent variable is simply the increase in explained variance brought about by left–right self-placement on discrete vote choices, the negative impact of 'post-communism' re-emerges. Left–right ideology seems to constitute a less useful cue for voters in these countries, even when levels of ideological polarization, congruence between left–right and anti- and pro-European positions and electoral system characteristics are taken into account.

These results deserve several comments. First, we know that different sets of coherent and integrated institutions are associated with different models of democracy (Lijphart 1999). However, there is wide institutional variation (concerning electoral system proportionality, degree of polarization and congruence between left–right and pro- and anti Europe positions of parties). Indeed, the differences between consolidating and established democracies remain even after controlling for the relevant variables concerning this attributes. Secondly, our results are congruent with prior research about the importance of the party (and political) system level of institutionalization for the anchoring of both party choice and political attitudes (Van der Brug and Franklin 2005; Mainwaring and Torcal 2005; Freire 2008a). Thirdly, the different results found between the multi-level linear regression (which imposed a dimension competition (left–right)) and the aggregate level regressions (which did not impose any dimension of competition) reveal that other dimensions of competition are also relevant (pro- and anti-European integration, libertarian–authoritarian or GAL-TAN — see below, etc.) and that, because of this, level of party (and political) system institutionalization is important even after controlling for the clarity of policy alternatives in the left–right dimension of competition. Although we know that left and right mean different things in different countries, and that they have a multidimensional character incorporating not only economic issues but also new politics issues (Knutsen 1997; Freire 2006b), the truth is that left and right are usually and above all correlated with attitudes towards economic issues. Thus, in a way, these results might also be an indicator that a significant part of political contestation over European integration is not only about economic interests but also about identities, especially in the new member states (Hooghe and Marks 2008, 18). Hooghe and Marks' hypothesis (2008, 18) gives a precious hint about what might be behind the differences we found between the consolidating democracies and the long-established democracies: 'Party conflict on European integration is simpler and more polarized in Central and Eastern Europe because gal/tan and left/right reinforce, rather than crosscut, each other. The axis of party competition that emerged after the collapse of communism runs from left-tan to right-gal, pitting market and cultural liberals against social protectionists and nationalists'.

Indeed, future research in this field should consider the relative strength of the left–right anchor as the main structuring factor of party competition *vis-à-vis* other dimensions that might be more important in structuring that competition. An important strand of the literature, driven by recent work on central and Eastern Europe has argued that parties compete in the European political space and/or in European elections not so much along the left–right axis as along the GAL (Green/Alternative/Libertarian)/TAN (Traditonal/Authoritarian/Nationalist) axis (Hooghe, Marks, and Wilson 2004). Importantly, this GAL/TAN axis is not congruent with the left–right positions of the parties in those systems. However, the EES 2004 questionnaire does not allow us to locate the parties (and the voters) on the GAL/TAN axis. Moreover, to the best of our knowledge there is no expert survey available (or data from party manifestos) that covers all the countries covered in this analysis. Whenever the available data allows, it would be crucial to test the impact of the contextual factors used in the present paper in a framework of policy competition (and electors' self-placement) structured by the GAL/TAN axis.

Acknowledgement

A previous version of this article was originally presented at the American Political Science Annual Meeting (APSA), 1–4 September 2005, Washington, DC: DIVISION 36-12 (Co-sponsored by DIVISION 15-21). The authors would like to thank Gary Marks (chair and discussant), as well as the other participants in that session (Hermann Schmitt, Michael Marsh, Mark

Franklin, Radoslaw Markwoski, Bernard Wessels, Jacques Thomassen and Richard Gunther) for their very insightful suggestions and criticisms that helped to improve the present revised version of the paper. More recently, an earlier version of the paper was presented at the EES Spring Meeting 2006 on The European Parliament Election of 2004, organized by the Institute of Social Sciences of the University of Lisbon (ICS), Lisbon, 12–13 May 2006. The authors would like to thank to all the participants in that session for their very insightful suggestions and criticisms that helped to improve the present revised version of the paper. This version was published as Freire, Lobo, and Magalhães (2007). Special thanks go to José Pereira and Edalina Sanches for valuable help in data management and analysis. Of course, all the problems that remain are the authors' exclusive responsibility.

Notes

1. The data utilized in this publication were originally collected by the 2004 European Election Study research group. The group consisted of Stefano Bartolini (EUI Florence, Italy), Cees van der Eijk (now University of Nottingham, UK), Mark Franklin (Trinity College, Hartford, Connecticut, USA), Dieter Fuchs (University of Stuttgart, GFR), Michael Marsh (Trinity College, Dublin, Ireland), Hermann Schmitt (University of Mannheim, GFR), and Gábor Toka (Central European University, Budapest, Hungary). This study was made possible by various grants. Neither the original collectors of the data nor their sponsors bear any responsibility for the analyses or interpretations published here. The data are still under embargo, except to the research directors referred to above, and the national research directors in each country. The authors of the present paper are the national research directors of EES 2004 in Portugal.

2. The only cases considered in the Van der Eijk, Schmitt, and Binder (2005) article were Germany, the Netherlands, Norway and Sweden.

3. Those who were still studying were recoded using the year of birth variable. Also France, Poland and Slovakia had a different coding for the education variable and these were harmonized.

4. See Lijphart (1994, 1999).

5. The interpolated median is computed in the following way. First, the variables are defined: M is the standard median of the responses; nl is the number of responses strictly less than M; ne is the number of responses equal to M; and ng is the number of responses strictly greater than M. Secondly, the interpolated median IM is then computed:

$$IM = M + (ng - nl) / (2ne) \qquad ne \text{ is non-zero}$$
$$IM = M \qquad ne \text{ is zero}$$

6. Traditionally, the arithmetic mean and the standard deviation (or some transformation of the latter) are used to describe such a frequency distribution in terms of central tendency and dispersion. In the case, of finite ordered rating scales these measures can be demonstrated to be biased (*by extreme values of the distribution*). With respect to the central tendency, see Huber and Powell (1994) and Herrera, Herrera, and Smith (1992), who recommended the interpolated median.

7. Similar measures of ideological distances at the party system level were used in Berglund et al. (2005), Knutsen and Kumlin (2005) and Freire (2006a, 2006b). When using voters' perceptions of parties' location in the left–right divide, the major differences *vis-à-vis* the present article is that they used the 'mean' for parties' locations and we used the 'interpolated median' value. We believe that the latter value is more accurate because, first, it is less sensitive to extreme values of the distribution and, secondly, it has got a more substantive meaning. See van der Eijk and Franklin (2004) for a different methodology.

8. The question (asked both for respondents' location and for parties' location) is stated in the following way: 'Some say European unification should be pushed further. Others say it already has gone too far. What is your opinion? Please indicate your views using a 10-point-scale. On this scale, 1

means unification "has already gone too far" and 10 means it "should be pushed further". What number on this scale best describes your position?'
9. Religiosity was coded in a five-point scale of mass attendance, from 1 (never) to 5 (several times a week). Social class is a (subjective) self-placement five-point scale, from 1 (working-class) to 5 (upper class). Education is a continuous variable capturing respondents' ages when they stopped studying (or current, if still studying).

References

Bartolini, Stefano. 2005. Les clivages politiques Européens. In *Dictionnaire des Élections Européennes*, ed. Yves Déloye, 98–108. Paris. Economica.
Bartolini, Stefano, and Peter Mair. 1990. *Identity, competition and electoral availability. The stabilisation of European electorates, 1885–1985*. Cambridge: Cambridge Univ. Press.
Berglund, Frode, Sören Holmberg, Hermann Schmitt, and Jacques Thomassen. 2005. Party identification and party choice. In Thomassen 2005, 106–24.
Brinegar, Adam P., Seth K. Jolly, and Herbert Kitschelt. 2004. Varieties of capitalism and political divides over European integration. In Marks and Steenbergen 2004, 62–92.
Downs, A. 1957. *An economic theory of democracy*. London: HarperCollins.
Farrell, David M., and Roger Scully. 2005. Electing the European Parliament: How uniform are 'uniform' electoral systems?. *Journal of Common Market Studies* 43: 969–84.
Franklin, Mark, Tom Mackie, and Henry Valen, eds. 1992. *Electoral change: Responses to evolving social and attitudinal structures in Western countries*. Cambridge: Cambridge Univ. Press.
Freire, André. 2006a. *Esquerda e Direita na Política Europeia: Portugal, Espanha e Grécia em Perspectiva Comparada*. Lisbon: Institute of Social Sciences/Imprensa de Ciências Sociais.
Freire, André. 2006b. Bringing social identities back in: The social anchors of left–right orientation in Western Europe. *International Political Science Review* 27, no. 4: 359–78.
Freire, André. 2008a. Left–right ideological identities in new democracies: Greece, Portugal and Spain in the Western European context. *Pôle Sud — Revue de Science Politique de l'Europe Méridionale* 25, no. II 2006: 153–73.
Freire, André. 2008b. Party polarization and citizens' left–right orientations. *Party Politics* 14, no. 2: 189–209.
Freire, André, Marina Costa Lobo, and Pedro Magalhães. 2007. Left–right and the European Parliament vote in 2004. In *European elections after Eastern Enlargement — Preliminary results from the European Election Study 2004*, eds. Michael Marsh, Slava Mikhaylov and Hermann Schmitt, 97–140. Germany: University of Mannheim, CONNEX Report Series N° 01, MZES.
Gabel, Matthew, and Simon Hix. 2004. Defining the EU political space: An empirical study of the European election manifestos, 1979–1999. In Marks and Steenbergen 2004, 93–119.
Gunther, R., and J.R. Montero. 2001. The anchors of partisanship: A comparative analysis of voting behaviour in four Southern European countries. In *Parties, politics, and democracy in new Southern Europe*, eds. N. Diamandouros and R. Gunther, 83–15. Baltimore, MD: The Johns Hopkins Univ. Press.
Herrera, C., R. Herrera, and E. Smith. 1992. Public opinion and congressional representation. *Public Opinion Quarterly* 56: 185–205.
Hix, Simon. 1999. Dimensions and alignments in European Union politics: Cognitive constraints and partisan responses. *European Journal of Political Research* 35, no. 1: 69–106.
Hix, Simon. 2005. Politics. In *The political system of the European Union*. 2nd ed, ed. Simon Hix, 147–234. Basingstoke: Palgrave Macmillan.
Hix, Simon, and Christopher Lord. 1997. *Political parties in the European Union*. New York: St Martin's Press.
Hooghe, Liesbet, and Gary Marks. 1999. The making of a polity: The struggle over European integration. In *Continuity and change in contemporary capitalism*, eds. H. Kitschelt, P. Lange, G. Marks, and J. Stephens, 70–97. Cambridge: Cambridge Univ. Press.
Hooghe, Liesbet, and Gary Marks. 2008. A postfunctionalist theory of European integration: From permissive consensus to constraining dissensus. *British Journal of Political Science* 39: 1–23.
Hooghe, Liesbet, Gary Marks, and Carole J. Wilson. 2004. Does left/right structure party positions on European integration? In Marks and Steenbergen 2004, 120–40.

Huber, J. 1989. Values and partisanship in left–right orientations: Measuring ideology. *European Journal of Political Research* 17: 599–621.

Huber, J., and G. Bingham Powell. 1994. Congruence between citizens and policymakers in two visions of liberal democracy. *World Politics* 46: 291–326.

Inglehart, Ronald, and Hans-Dieter Klingemann. 1976. Party identification, ideological preference and the left–right dimension among western mass publics. In *Party identification and beyond: Representations of voting and party competition,* eds. I. Budge, I. Crewe and D. Farlie, 243–76. London: John Wiley & Sons.

Kitschelt, Herbert, Zdenka Mansfeldova, Radoslaw Markowski, and Gábor Toka. 1999. *Postcommunist party systems. Competition, representation, and inter-party cooperation.* Cambridge: Cambridge Univ. Press.

Knutsen, Oddbjørn. 1995. Value orientations, political conflicts and left–right identification: A comparative study. *European Journal of Political Research* 28: 63–93.

Knutsen, Oddbjørn. 1997. The partisan and the value-based components of left–right self-placement: A comparative study. *International Political Science Review* 18: 191–225.

Knutsen, Oddbjørn, and Staffan Kumlin. 2005. Value orientations and party choice. In Thomassen 2005, 125–66.

Lawson, K., A. Rommele, and G. Karasimeonov, eds. 1999. *Cleavages, parties and voters: Studies from Bulgaria, the Czech Republic, Poland and Romania.* London: Praeger.

Lijphart, Arend, ed. 1994. *Electoral systems and party systems. A study of twenty-seven democracies 1945–1990.* Oxford: Oxford Univ. Press.

Lijphart, Arend. 1999. *Patterns of democracy: Government forms and performance in 36 countries.* New Haven, CT: Yale Univ. Press.

Mainwaring, Scott P. 1999. *Rethinking party systems in the third wave of democratization: The case of Brazil.* Stanford: Stanford Univ. Press.

Mainwaring, Scott P., and Mariano Torcal. 2005. Party system theory and party system institutionalization after the third wave of democratization. Paper presented at the Political Science Seminar of the Social Sciences Institute of the University of Lisbon, Portugal.

Marks, Gary. 2004. Conclusion: European integration and political conflict. In Marks and Steenbergen 2004, 235–59.

Marks, Gary, and Marco R. Steenbergen, eds. 2004. *European integration and political conflict.* Cambridge: Cambridge Univ. Press.

Nie, Norman H., and Kristi Andersen. 1974. Mass belief systems revisited: Political change and attitude structure. *Journal of Politics* 36: 540–87.

Norris, Pippa. 2004. *Electoral engineering: Voting rules and political behavior.* Cambridge: Cambridge Univ. Press.

Ray, Leonard. 2004. Don't rock the boat: Expectations, fears, and opposition to EU-level of policy making. In Marks and Steenbergen 2004, 51–61.

Sani, G., and G. Sartori. 1983. Polarization, fragmentation and competition in Western democracies. In *Western European party systems: Continuity and change,* eds. H. Daalder and P. Mair, 307–40. London: Sage.

Sartori, G. 1992 [1976]. *Partidos y Sistemas de Partidos.* Madrid: Alianza Editorial.

Schmitt, Herman, and Jacques Thomassen, eds. 1999. *Political representation and legitimacy in the European Union.* Oxford: Oxford Univ. Press.

Steenbergen, Marco R., and Gary Marks. 2004. Introduction: Models of political conflict in the European Union. In Marks and Steenbergen 2004, 1–12.

Steenbergen, Marco R., and David J. Scott. 2004. Contesting Europe? The salience of European integration as a party issue. In Marks and Steenbergen 2004.

Taggart, Paul. 1998. A touchstone of dissent: Euroskepticism in contemporary West European party systems. *European Journal of Political Research* 33: 363–88.

Taggart, Paul, and Aleks Szczerbiak. 2004. Contemporary Euroskepticism in the party systems of European Union candidate states of Central and Eastern Europe. *European Journal of Political Research* 43: 1–27.

Thomassen, Jacques. 2005. *The European voter. A comparative study of modern democracies.* Oxford: Oxford Univ. Press.

Thomassen, Jacques, Abdul Noury, and Erik Voeten. 2004. Political competition in the European Parliament: Evidence from roll call and survey analyses. In Marks and Steenbergen 2004.

Tsebelis, George, and Geoffrey Garret. 2000. Legislative politics in the European Union. *European Union Politics* 1: 9–36.

Van der Brug, Wouter, and Cees Van der Eijk. 1999. The cognitive basis of voting. In Schmitt and Thomassen 1999, 129–60.

Van der Brug, Wouter, and Mark Franklin. 2005. One electorate or many? Testing the distinctiveness of electoral behavior in new and established member states during the 2004 elections to the European Parliament. Paper delivered at the conference on the 2004 European Parliament Elections, May, Budapest, Hungary.

Van der Eijk, Cees, and Mark Franklin. 2004. Potential for contestation on European matters at national elections in Europe. In Marks and Steenbergen 2004, 32–50.

Van der Eijk, Cees, Mark Franklin, and Wouter van der Brug. 1999. Policy preferences and party choice. In Schmitt and Thomassen 1999, 161–85.

Van der Eijk, Cees, Mark Franklin, and Erik Oppenhuis. 1996. The strategic context: Party choice. In Van der Eijk and Franklin 1996, 332–65.

Van der Eijk, Cees, Hermann Schmitt, and Tanja Binder. 2005. Left–right orientations and party choice. In Thomassen 2005, 167–91.

White, S., R. Rose, and I. McAllister. 1997. *How Russia votes.* Chatham, NJ: Chatham House.

Index

Page numbers in *Italics* represent tables.